BUTCH AND PETEY ARE LONG-HAUL TRUCKERS. THEY'VE BEEN DRIVING COAST-TO-COAST IN THE SAME TRUCK FOR THE SAME COMPANY FOR NEARLY A DOZEN YEARS.

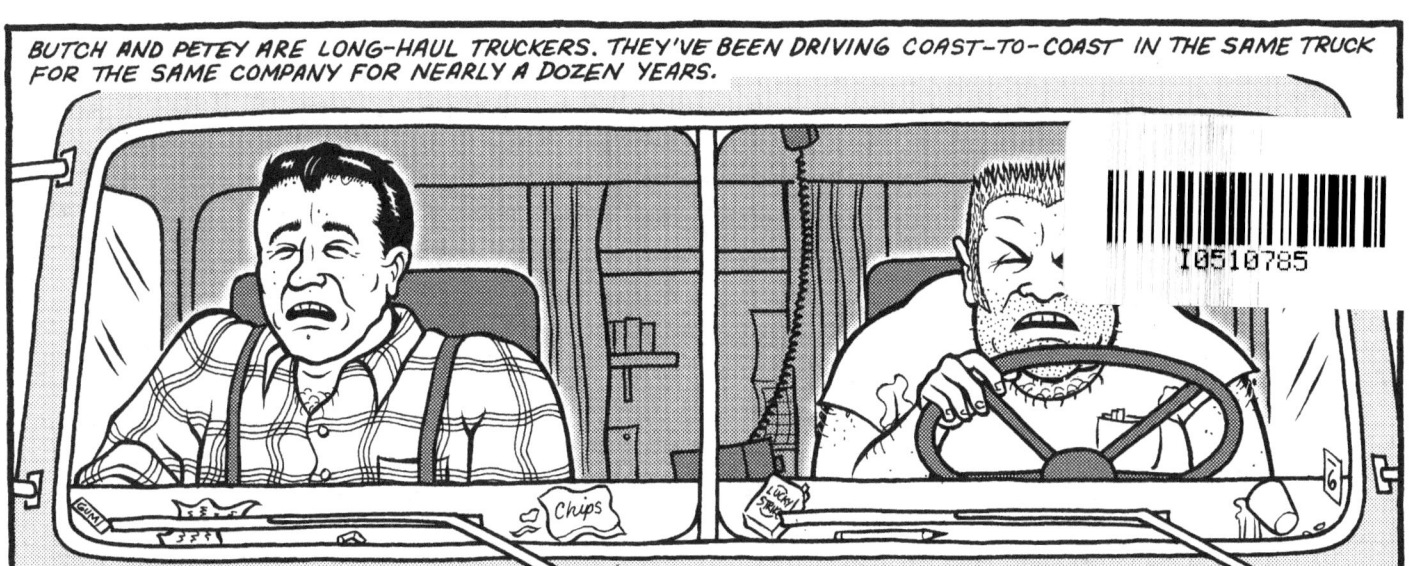

BUTCH IS THE ALPHA MALE OF THIS TWO-MAN TRUCKER WOLFPACK. HE TENDS TO BULLY THE SIMPLER, SOFTER PETEY. A CRUSTY, REMORSELESS MAN, HE IS A REPOSITORY OF USELESS INFORMATION AND NARROW-MINDED OPINIONS.

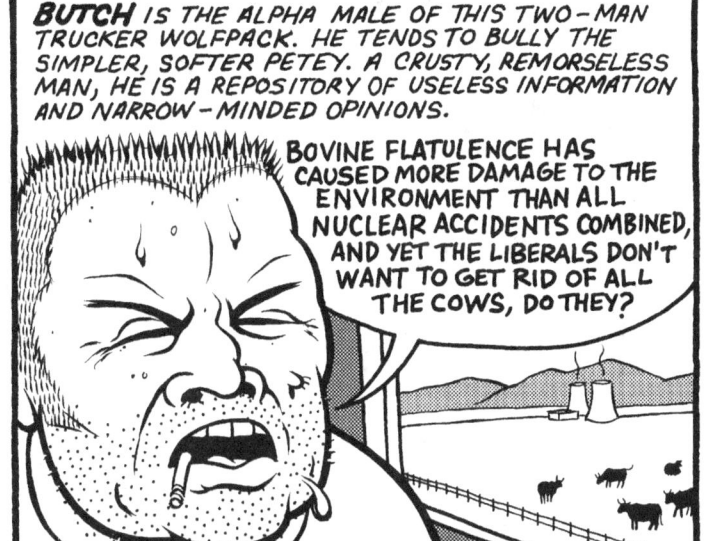

BOVINE FLATULENCE HAS CAUSED MORE DAMAGE TO THE ENVIRONMENT THAN ALL NUCLEAR ACCIDENTS COMBINED, AND YET THE LIBERALS DON'T WANT TO GET RID OF ALL THE COWS, DO THEY?

PETEY IS BLESSED WITH THE KIND HEART AND SUPER-HUMAN STRENGTH OF A BORDERLINE RETARDATE.

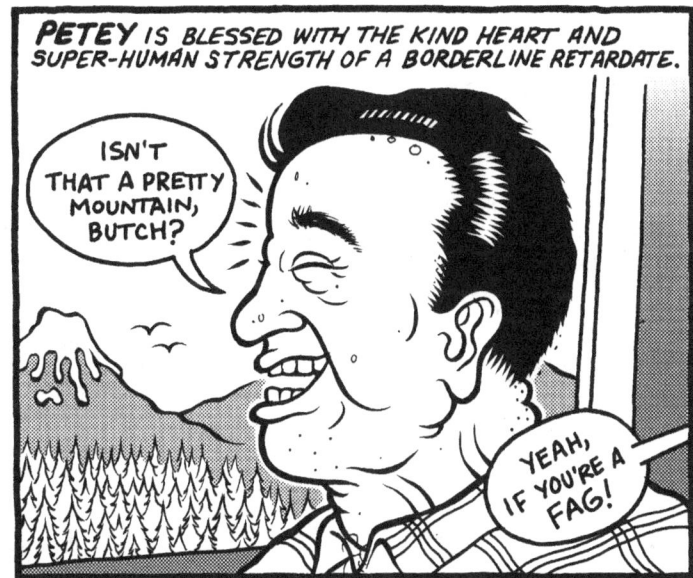

ISN'T THAT A PRETTY MOUNTAIN, BUTCH?

YEAH, IF YOU'RE A FAG!

TO PUT IT KINDLY, BUTCH AND PETEY ARE PAST THEIR PRIME. IT HAS BEEN MORE THAN A DECADE SINCE EITHER OF THEM HAS HAD CONSENSUAL, NON-PAYING SEX WITH A WOMAN.

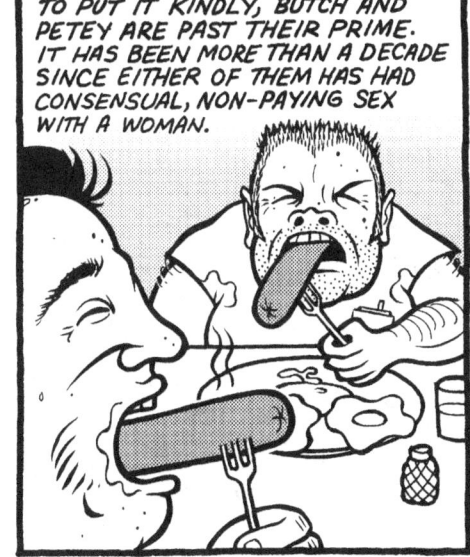

BUTCH AND PETEY SPEND MORE TIME TOGETHER THAN MOST MARRIED COUPLES. THEY SPEND PERHAPS MORE TIME TOGETHER THAN ANY TWO MEN SHOULD.

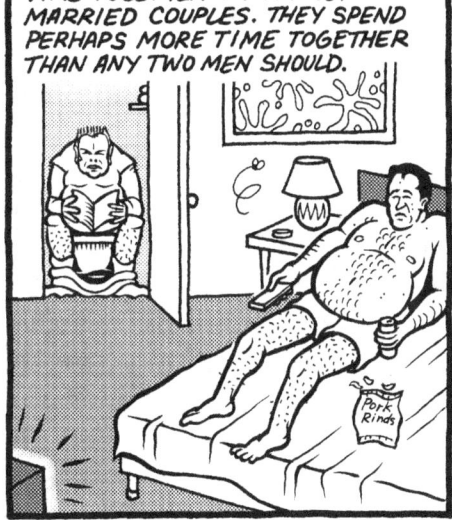

AND SOMETIMES THE ROAD GETS VERY, VERY LONELY.

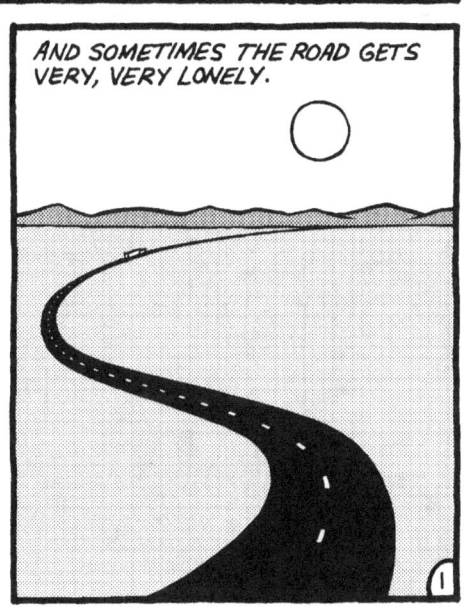

1

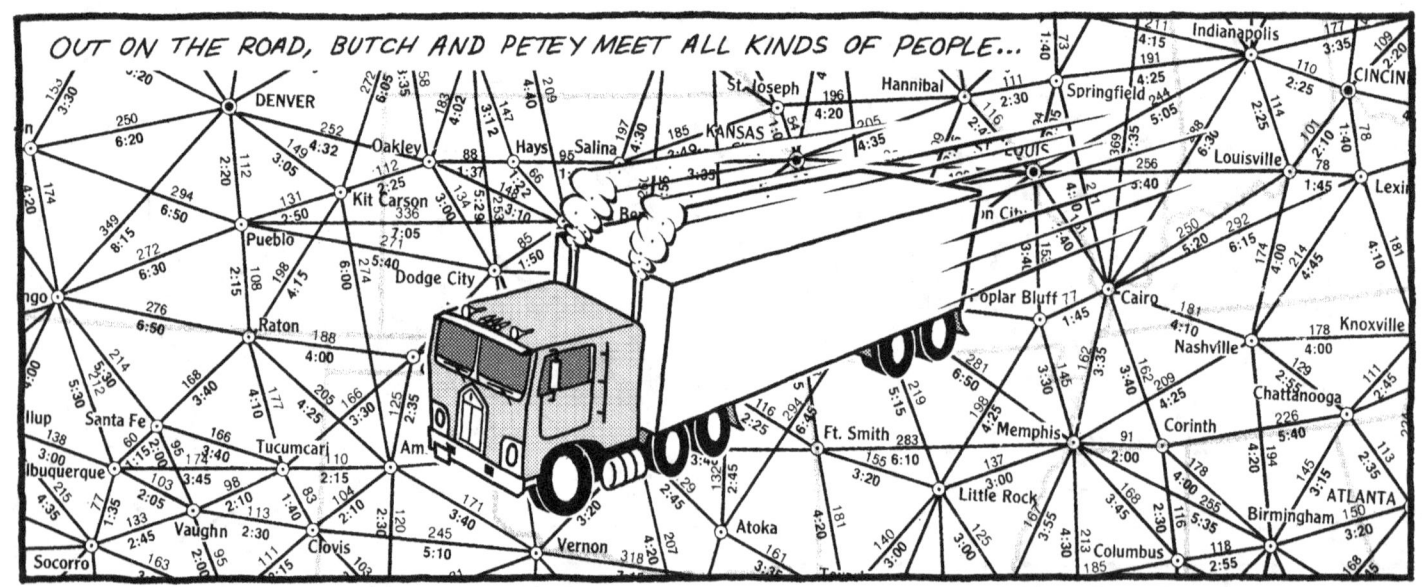

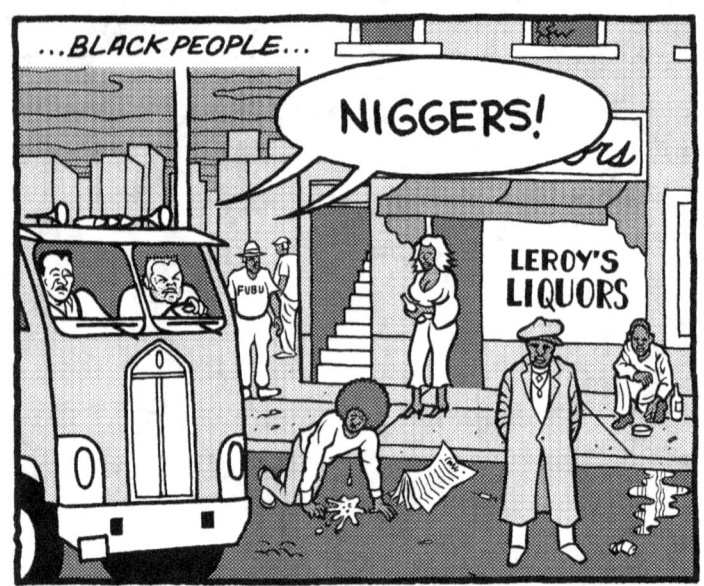

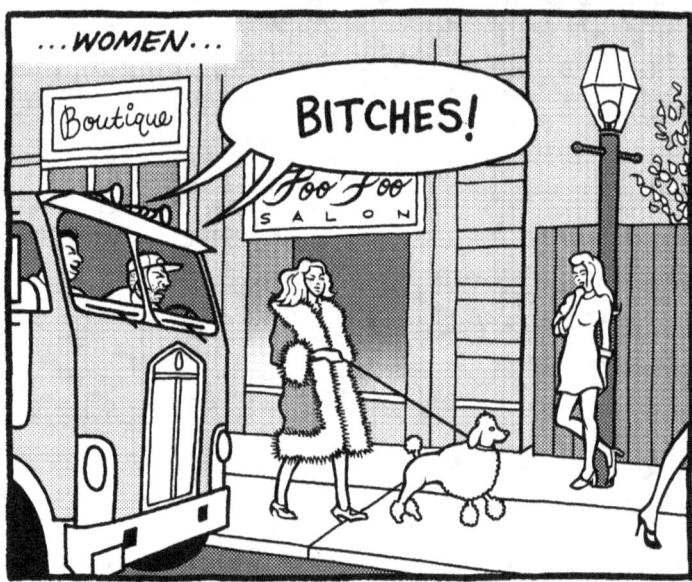

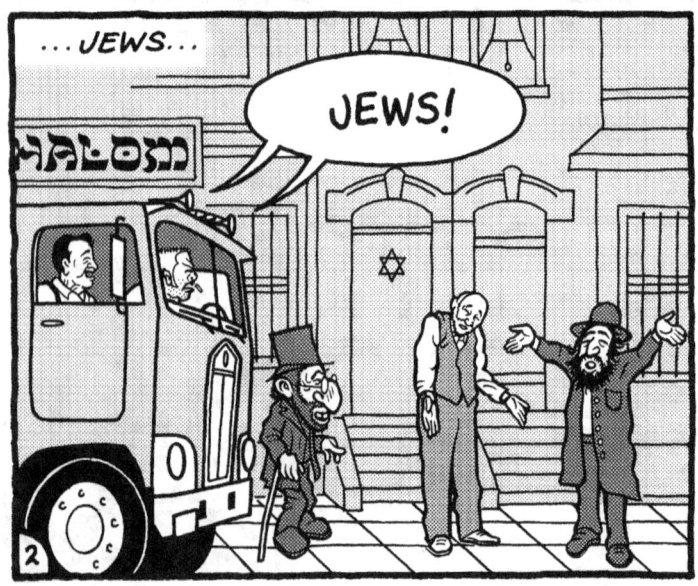

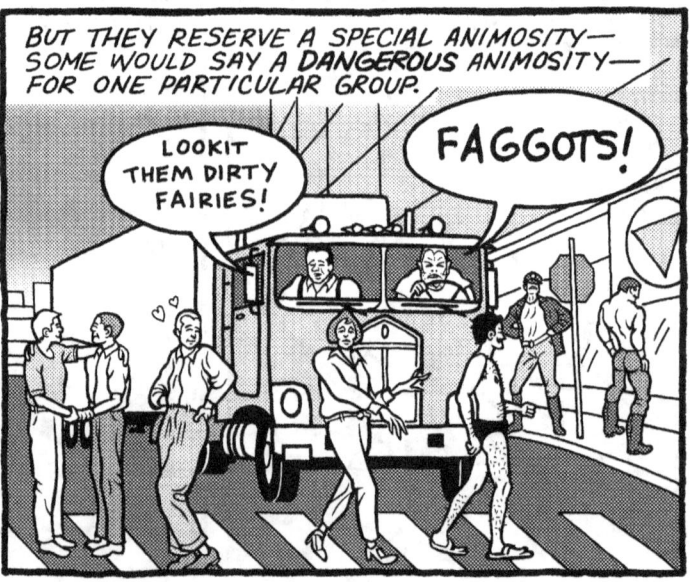

PERSONS WITH AN IRRATIONAL FEAR AND/OR HATRED OF HOMOSEXUALS ARE KNOWN AS **HOMOPHOBES**. THEIR ATTITUDES ARE THOUGHT TO BE ROOTED IN THEIR OWN REPRESSED FEARS OF BEING HOMOSEXUAL.

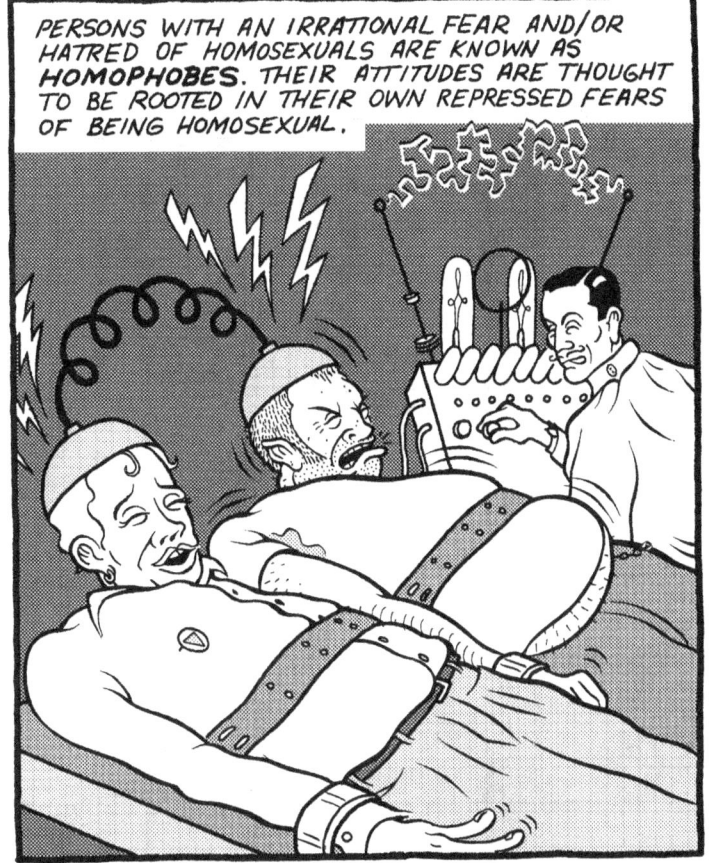

BUT ALTHOUGH BUTCH AND PETEY MIGHT ADMIT TO **HATING** HOMOSEXUALS, THEY'D NEVER COP TO **FEARING** THEM.

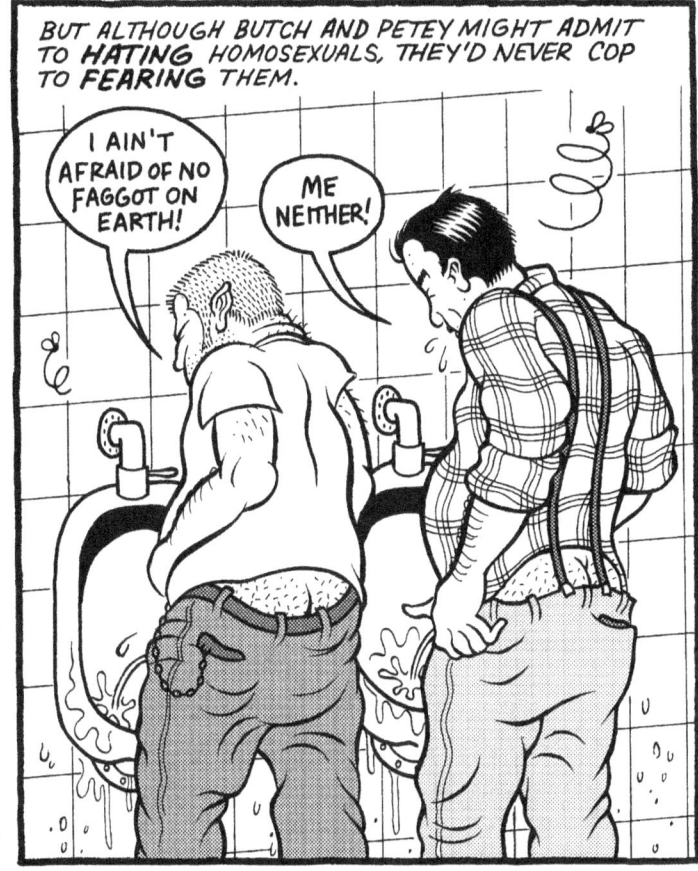

I AIN'T AFRAID OF NO FAGGOT ON EARTH!

ME NEITHER!

BUTCH AND PETEY HAVE A SIMPLE PLAN FOR DEALING WITH WHAT THEY CALL "THE HOMO-SEXUAL PROBLEM."

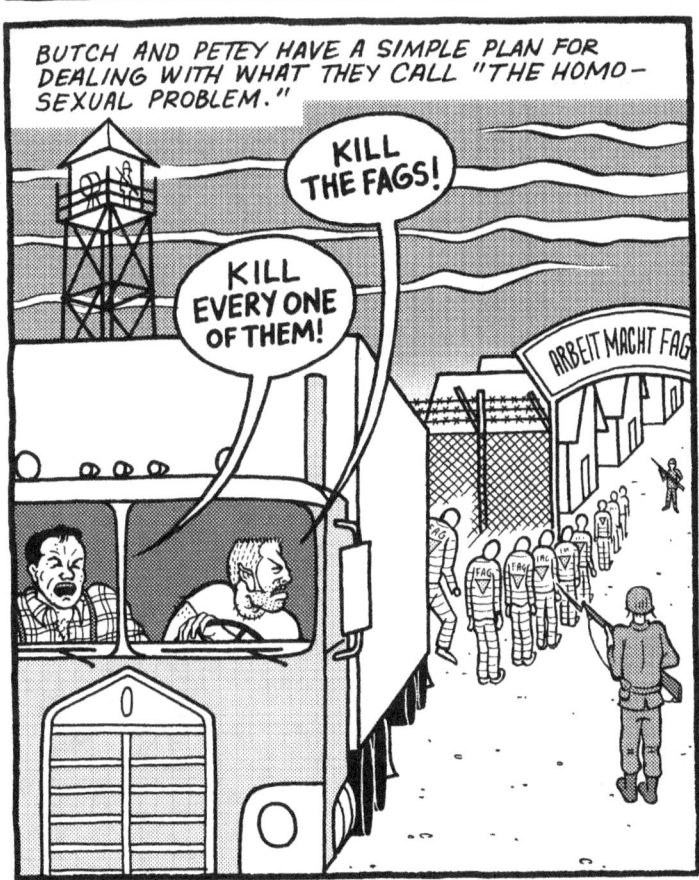

KILL THE FAGS!

KILL EVERY ONE OF THEM!

ARBEIT MACHT FAG

BUT IN TODAY'S CHANGING WORLD, THERE ARE THOSE WHO QUESTION THE MORALITY OF SUCH A HARD-LINE ANTI-HOMO STANCE.

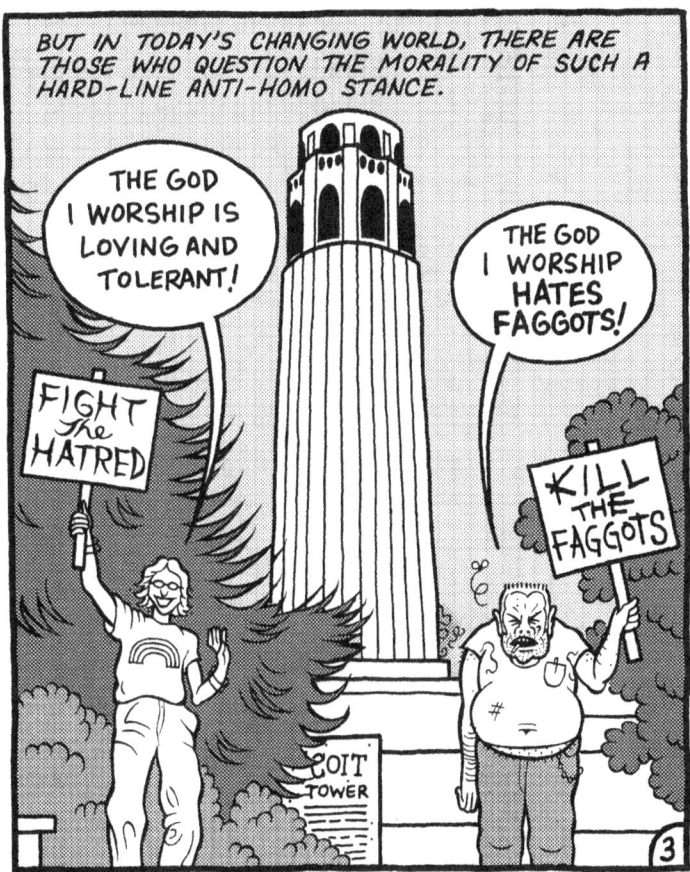

THE GOD I WORSHIP IS LOVING AND TOLERANT!

THE GOD I WORSHIP HATES FAGGOTS!

FIGHT the HATRED

KILL THE FAGGOTS

COIT TOWER

③

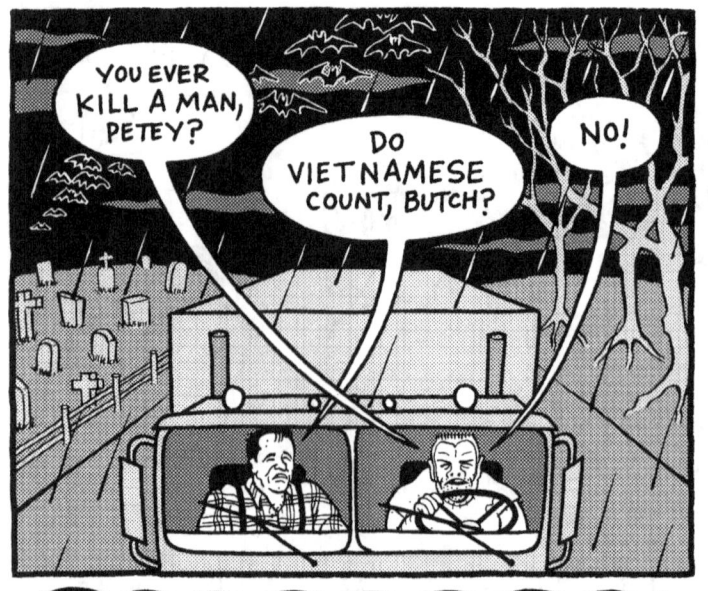

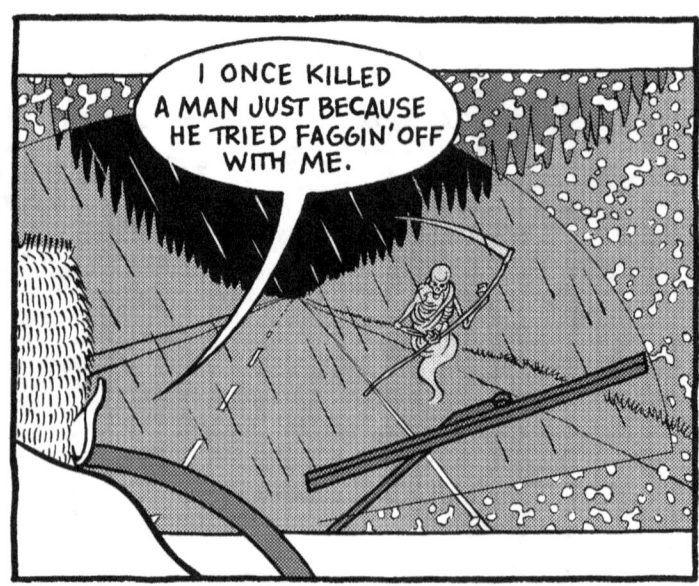

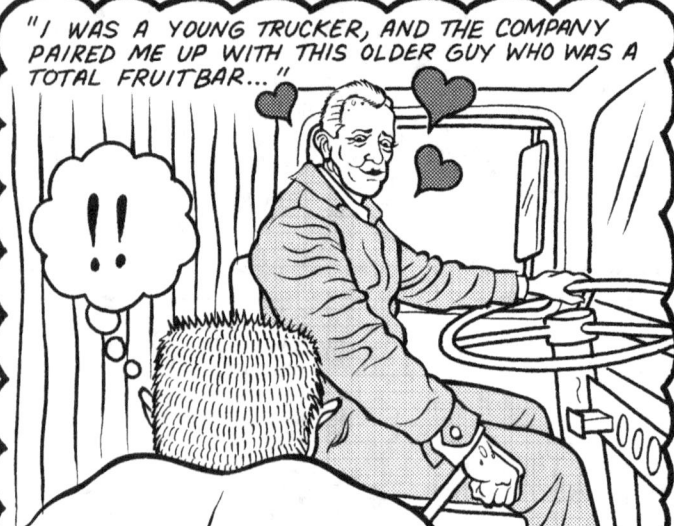

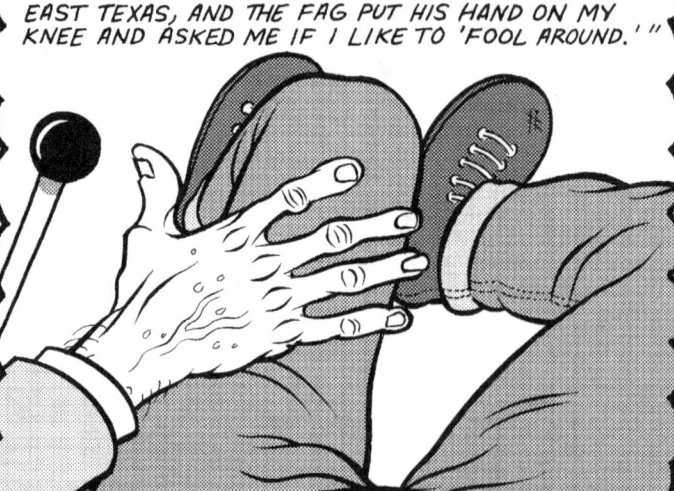

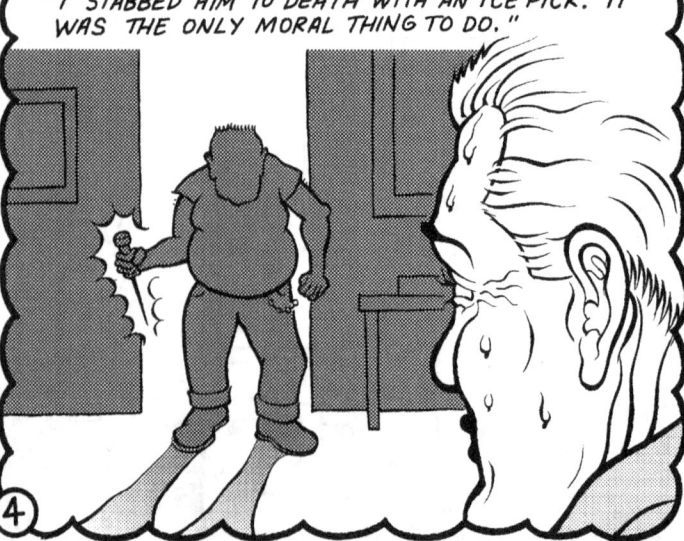

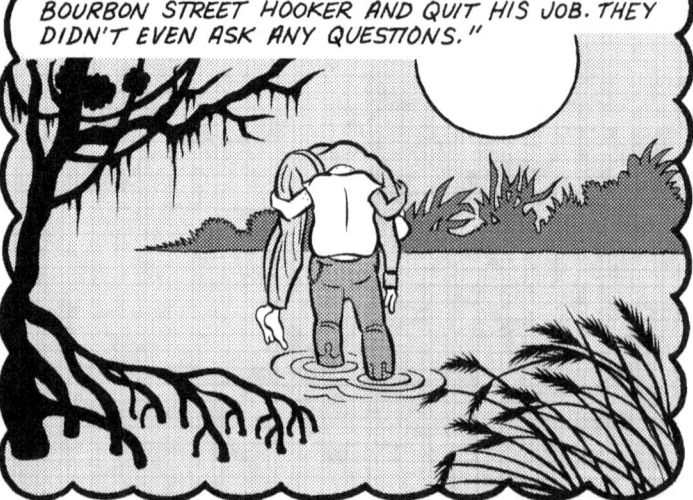

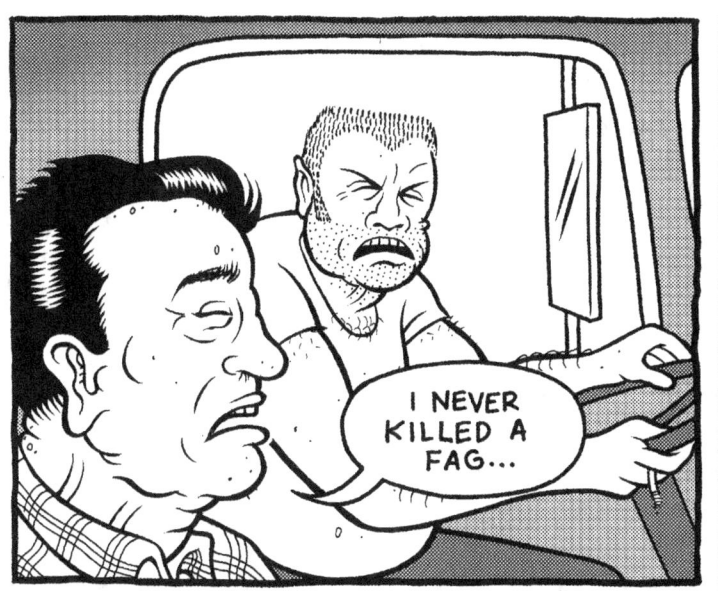

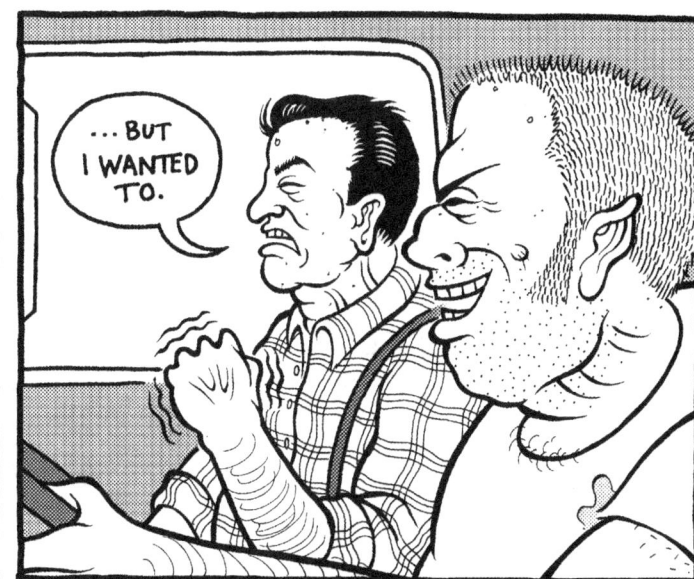

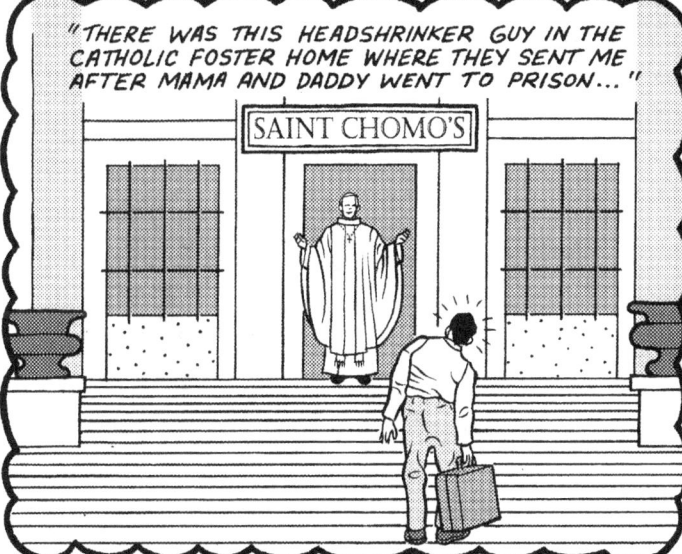

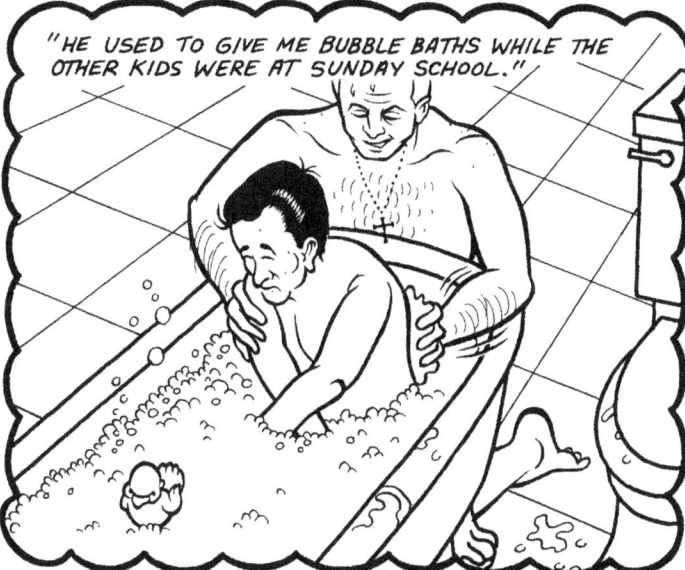

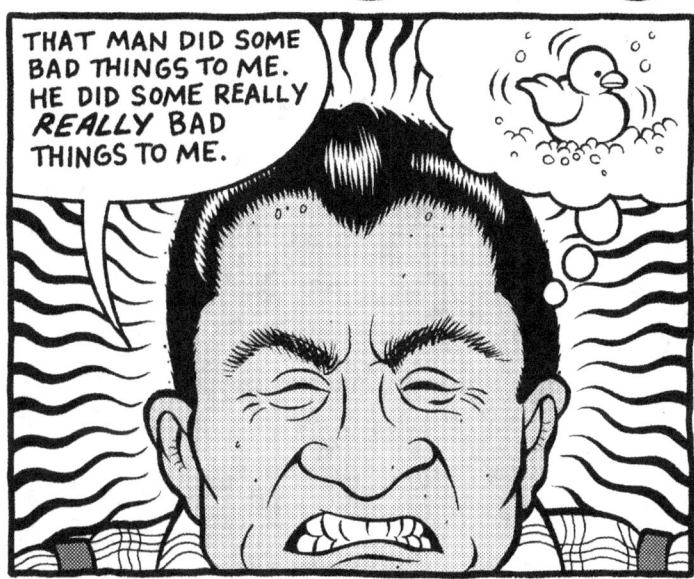

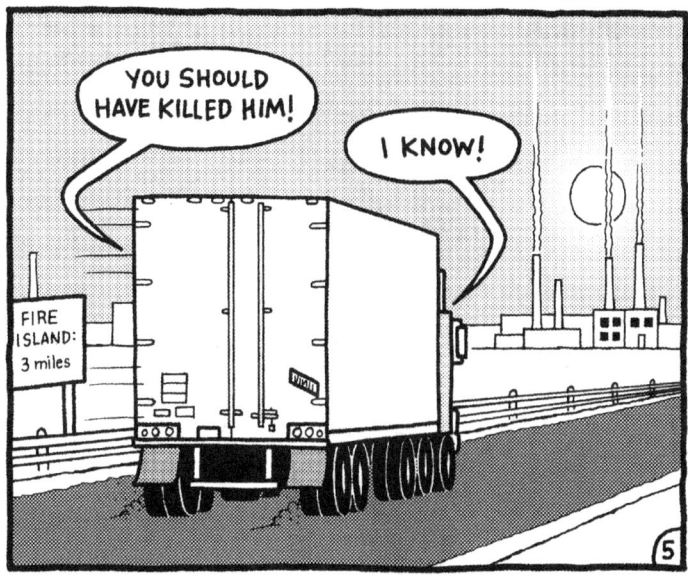

TO THE CASUAL OBSERVER, IT WOULD SEEM THAT BUTCH AND PETEY TALK MORE ABOUT KILLING HOMOSEXUALS THAN THEY DO ABOUT HAVING SEX WITH WOMEN.

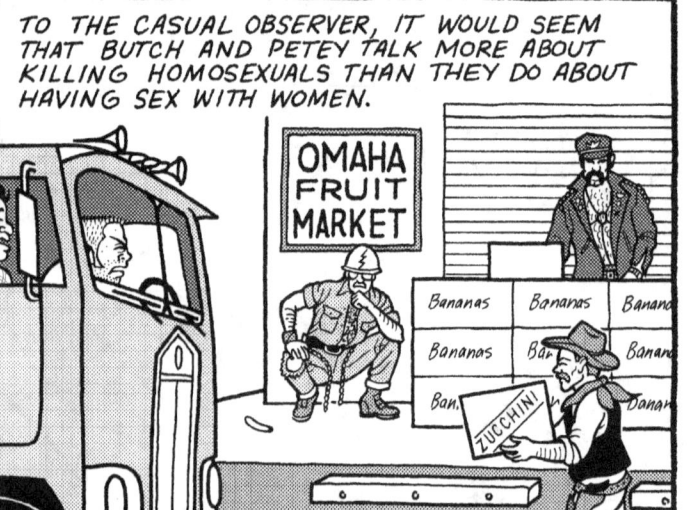

WOMEN DO NOT FIND BUTCH AND PETEY SEXUALLY ATTRACTIVE. HOMELY, OBESE, AGING, HATE-FILLED GRUNT WORKERS HOLD LITTLE APPEAL FOR THE LADIES.

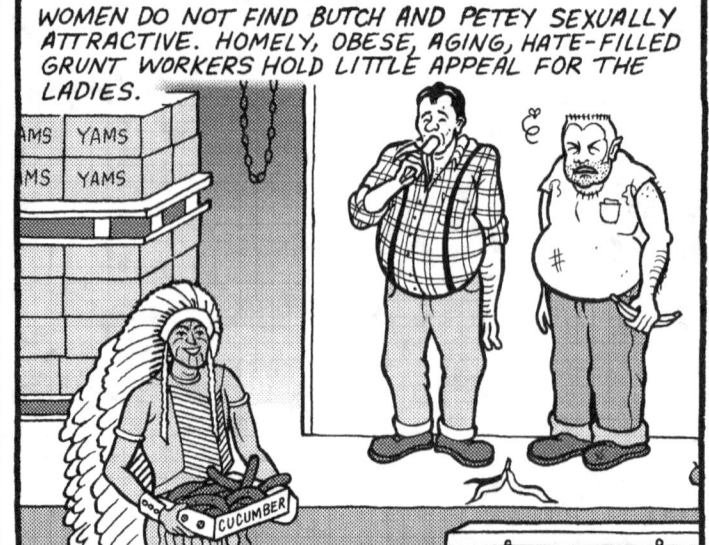

BUTCH AND PETEY HAVE BEEN LIFELONG BACHELORS. THEIR RELATIONSHIPS WITH WOMEN HAVE BEEN BRIEF, INFREQUENT, AND DISASTROUS.

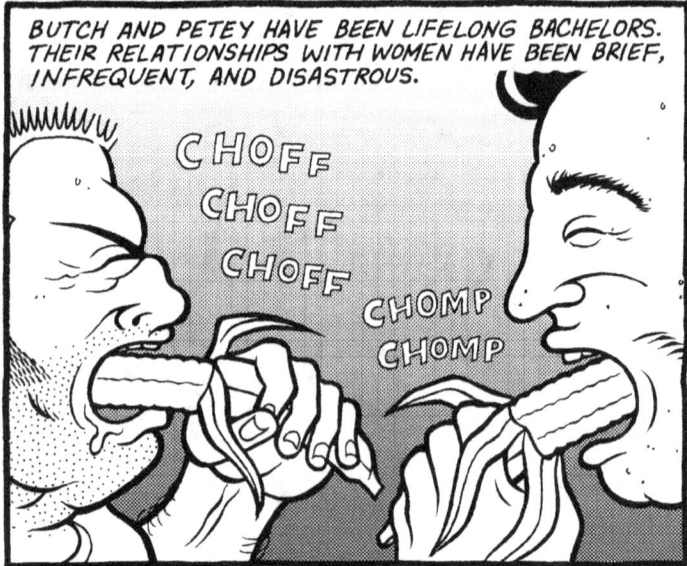

BUTCH HAS HAD SEXUAL INTERCOURSE WITH EIGHT WOMEN IN HIS LIFE. THREE OF THEM WERE PROSTITUTES. OF THE 12,773 ORGASMS HE'S HAD IN HIS LIFE, ALL BUT 233 OF THEM WERE FROM MASTURBATION.

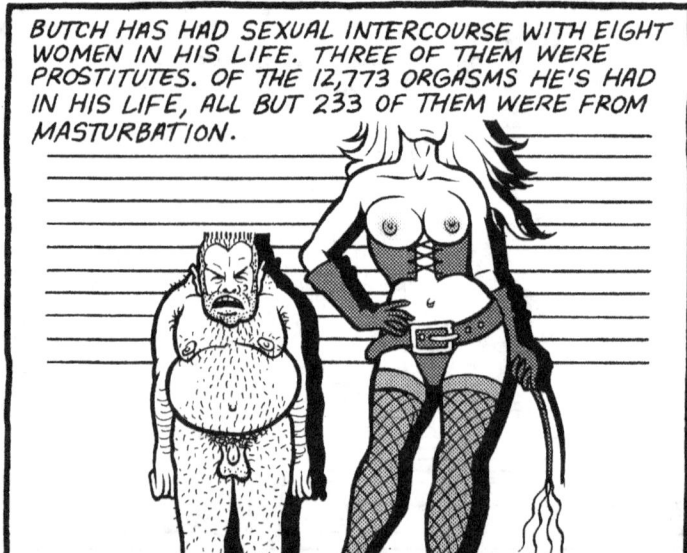

PETEY HAS HAD SEXUAL INTERCOURSE WITH FIVE WOMEN IN HIS LIFE. FOUR OF THEM WERE PROSTITUTES. OF THE 18,662 ORGASMS HE'S HAD IN HIS LIFE, ALL BUT 19 OF THEM WERE FROM MASTURBATION.

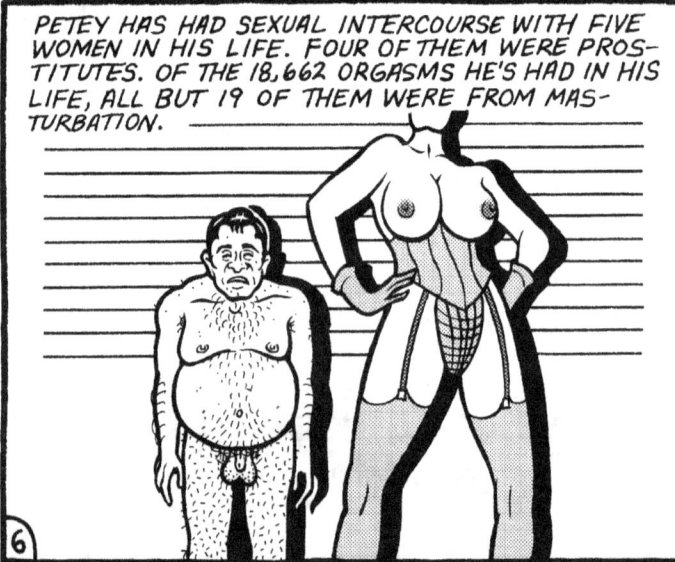

FOR TWO MEN SO STRIDENTLY OPPOSED TO ALL FORMS OF FAGGOTRY, BUTCH AND PETEY ARE SORRY EXCUSES FOR HETEROSEXUALS.

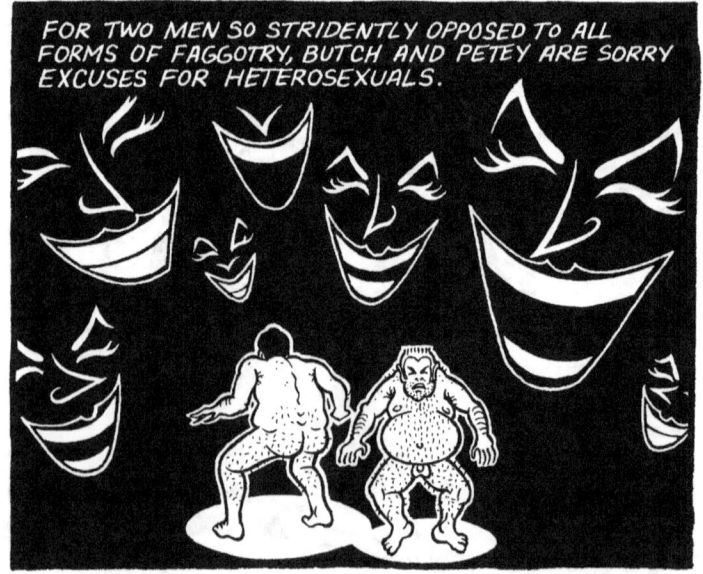

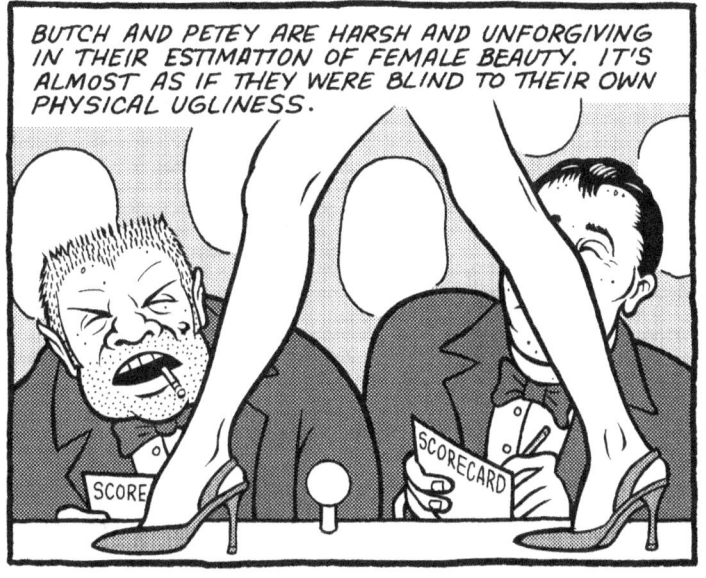

BUTCH AND PETEY ARE HARSH AND UNFORGIVING IN THEIR ESTIMATION OF FEMALE BEAUTY. IT'S ALMOST AS IF THEY WERE BLIND TO THEIR OWN PHYSICAL UGLINESS.

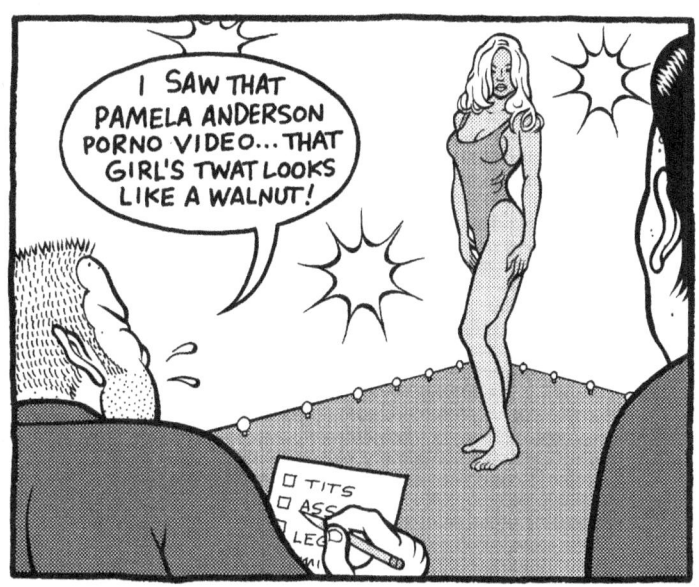

I SAW THAT PAMELA ANDERSON PORNO VIDEO... THAT GIRL'S TWAT LOOKS LIKE A WALNUT!

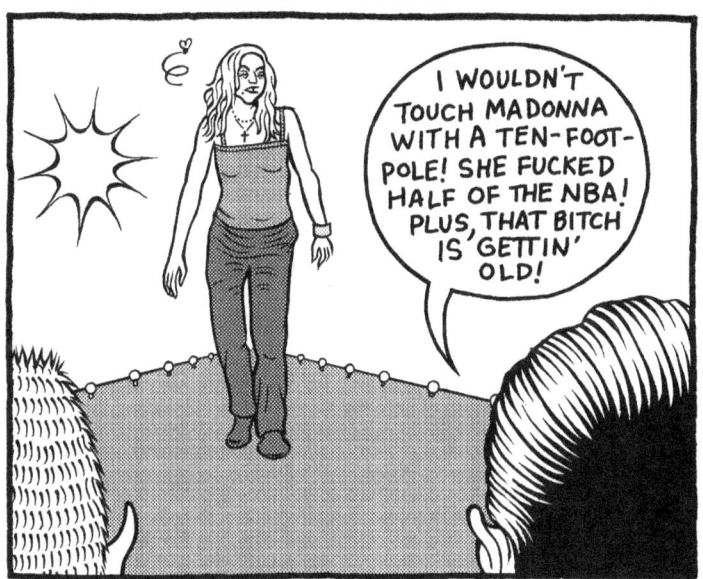

I WOULDN'T TOUCH MADONNA WITH A TEN-FOOT-POLE! SHE FUCKED HALF OF THE NBA! PLUS, THAT BITCH IS GETTIN' OLD!

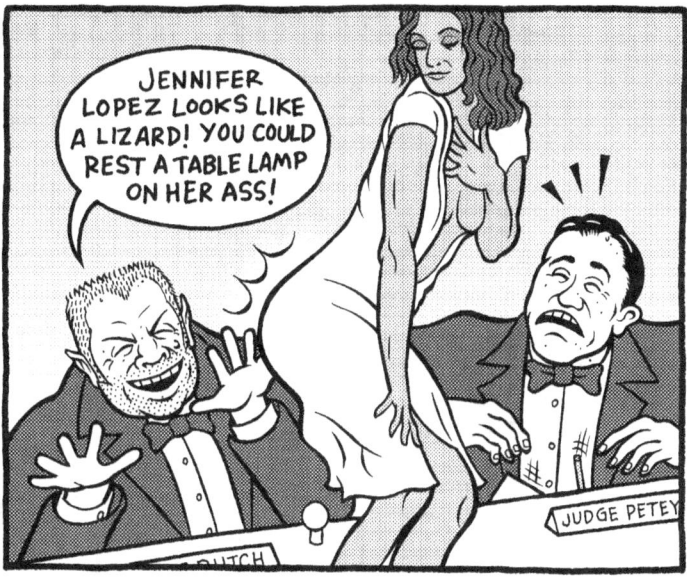

JENNIFER LOPEZ LOOKS LIKE A LIZARD! YOU COULD REST A TABLE LAMP ON HER ASS!

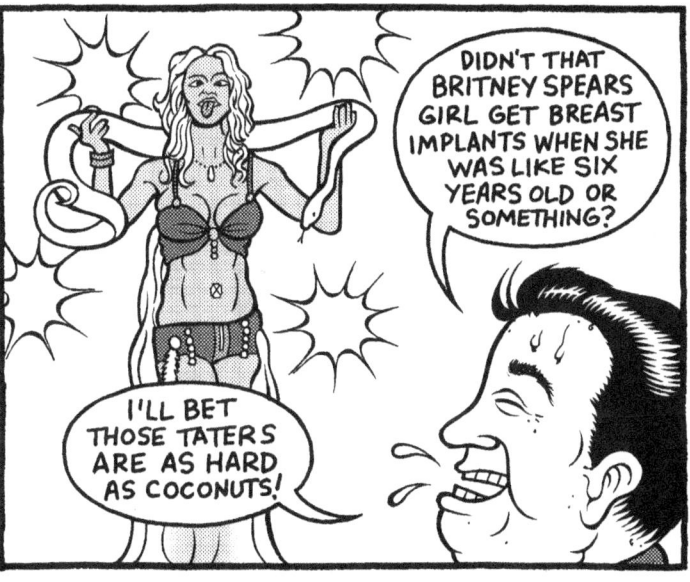

DIDN'T THAT BRITNEY SPEARS GIRL GET BREAST IMPLANTS WHEN SHE WAS LIKE SIX YEARS OLD OR SOMETHING?

I'LL BET THOSE TATERS ARE AS HARD AS COCONUTS!

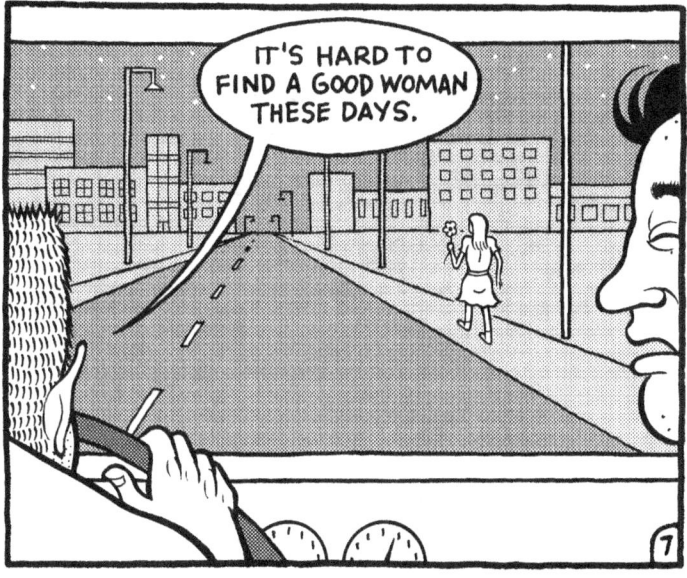

IT'S HARD TO FIND A GOOD WOMAN THESE DAYS.

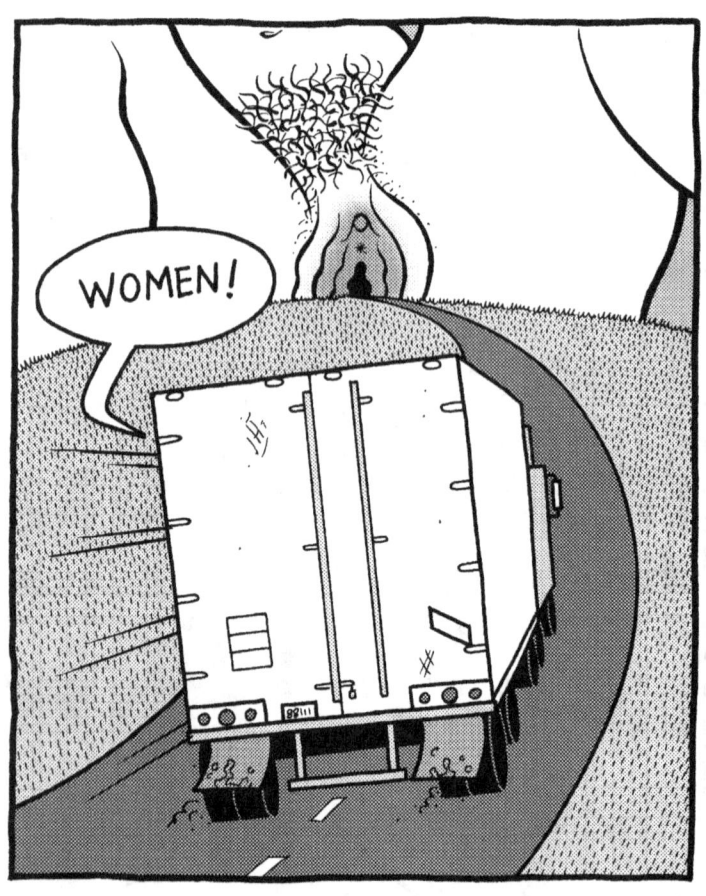

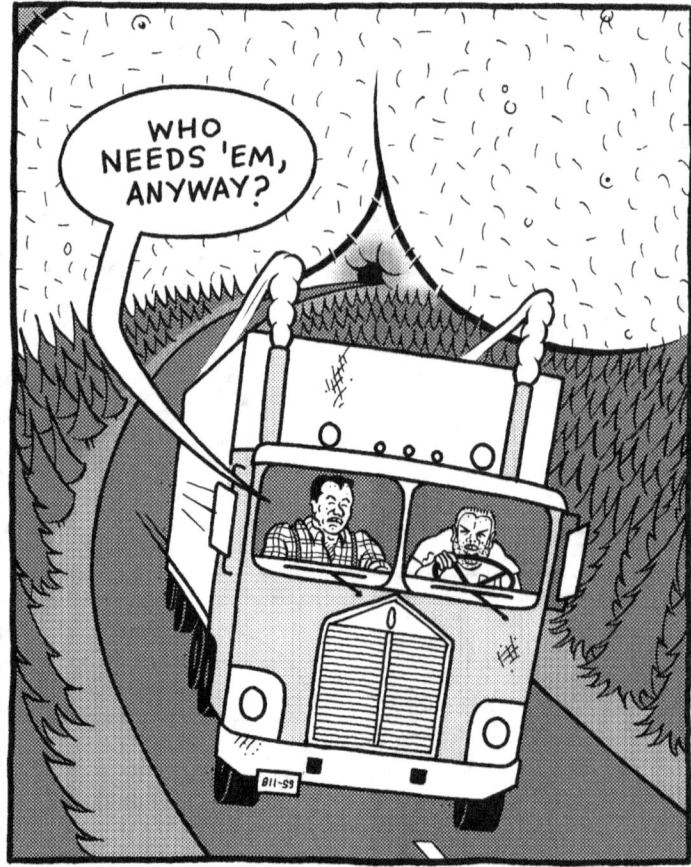

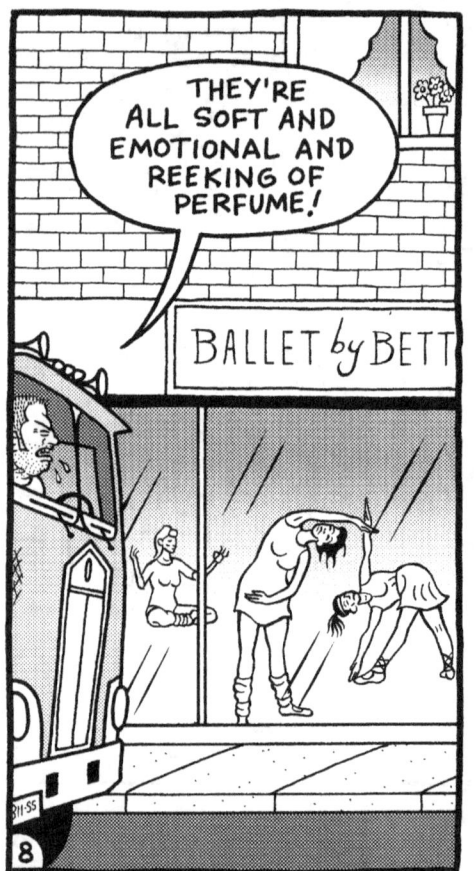

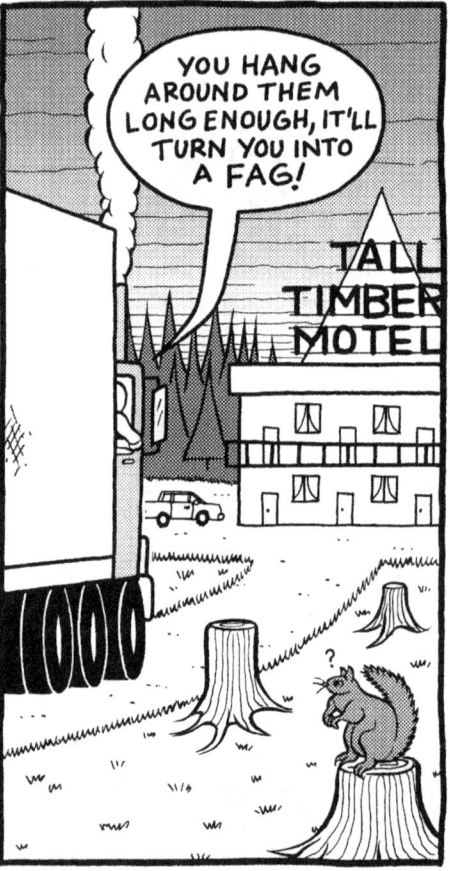

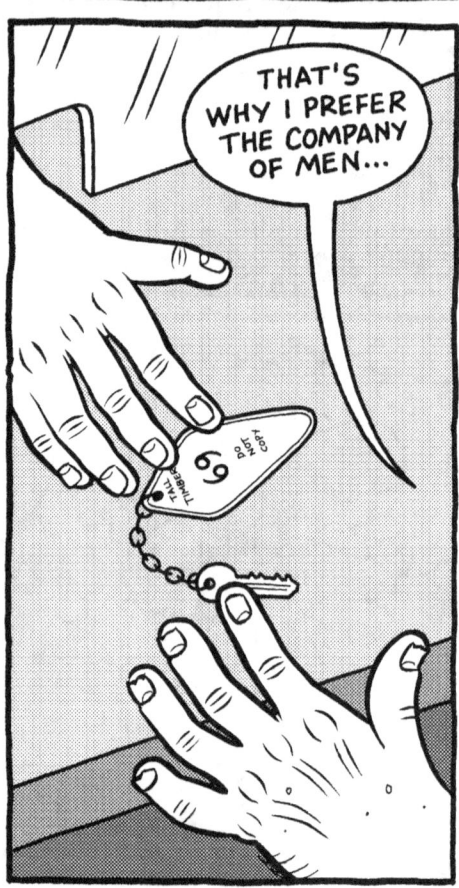

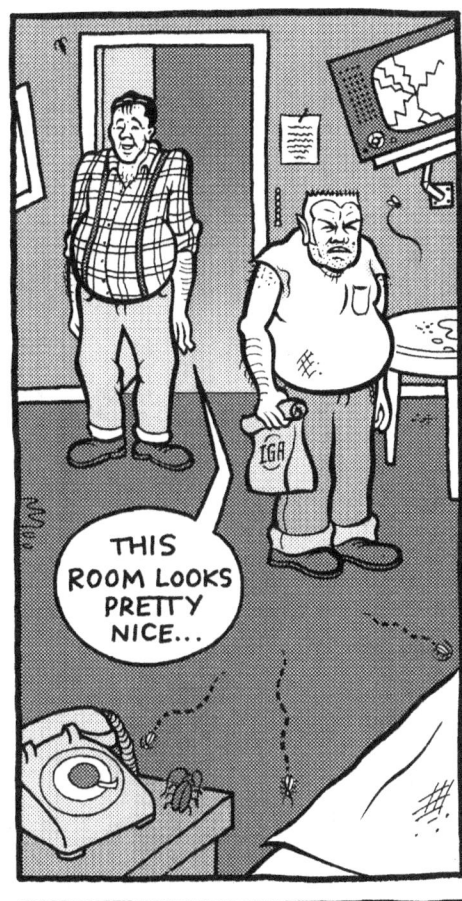

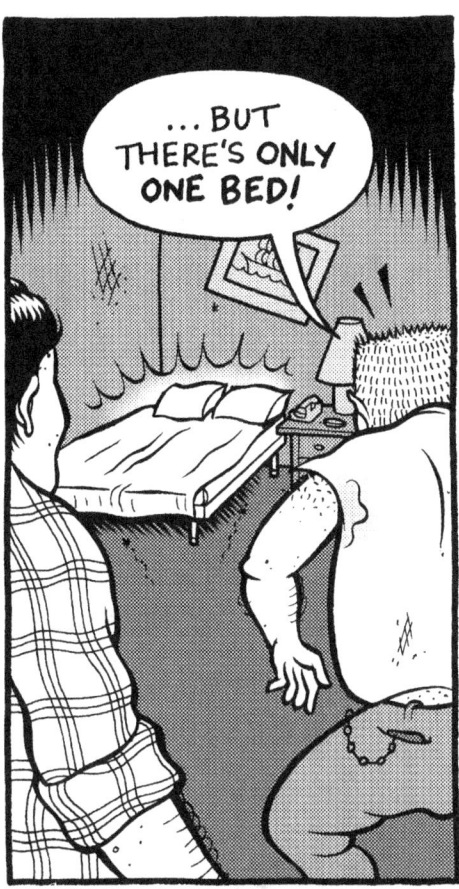

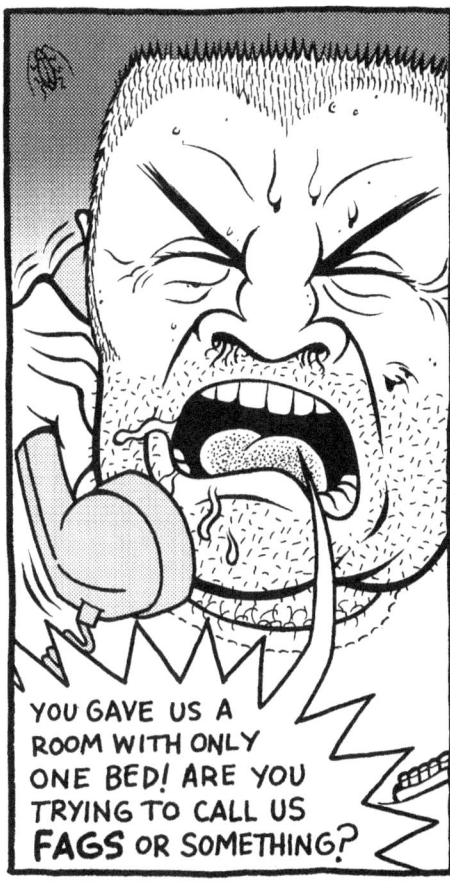

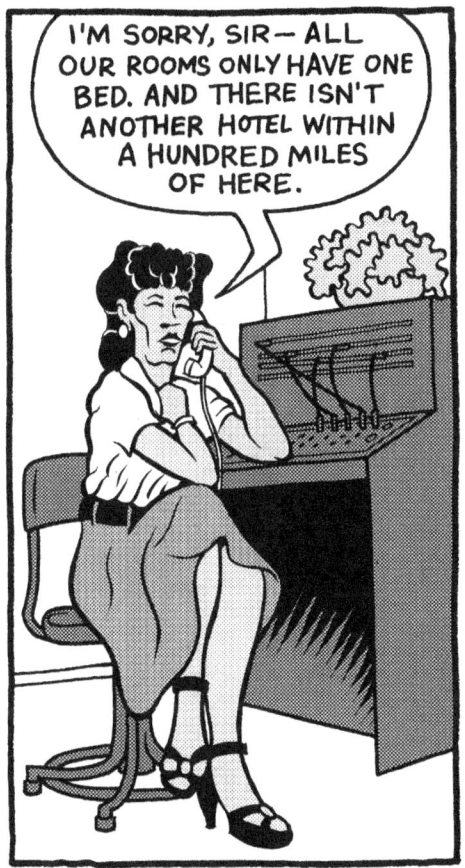

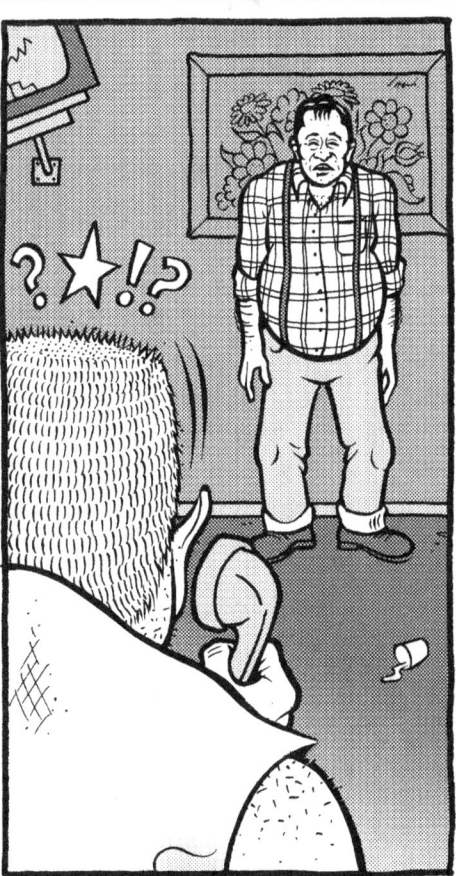

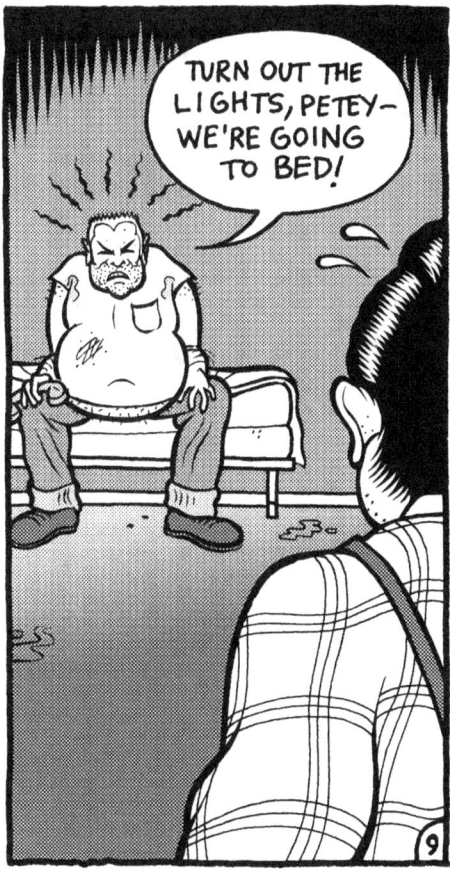

9

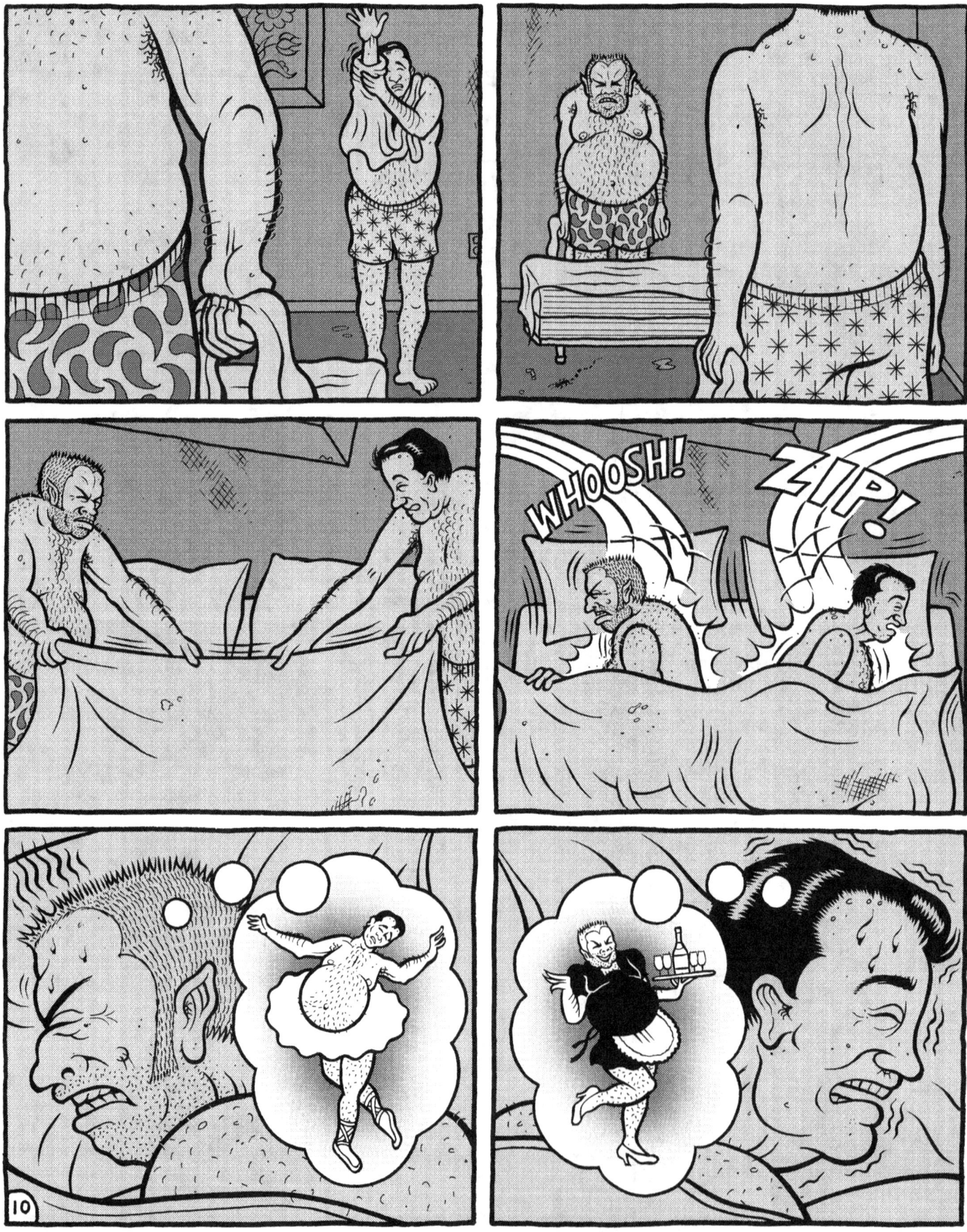

WHOOSH! ZIP!

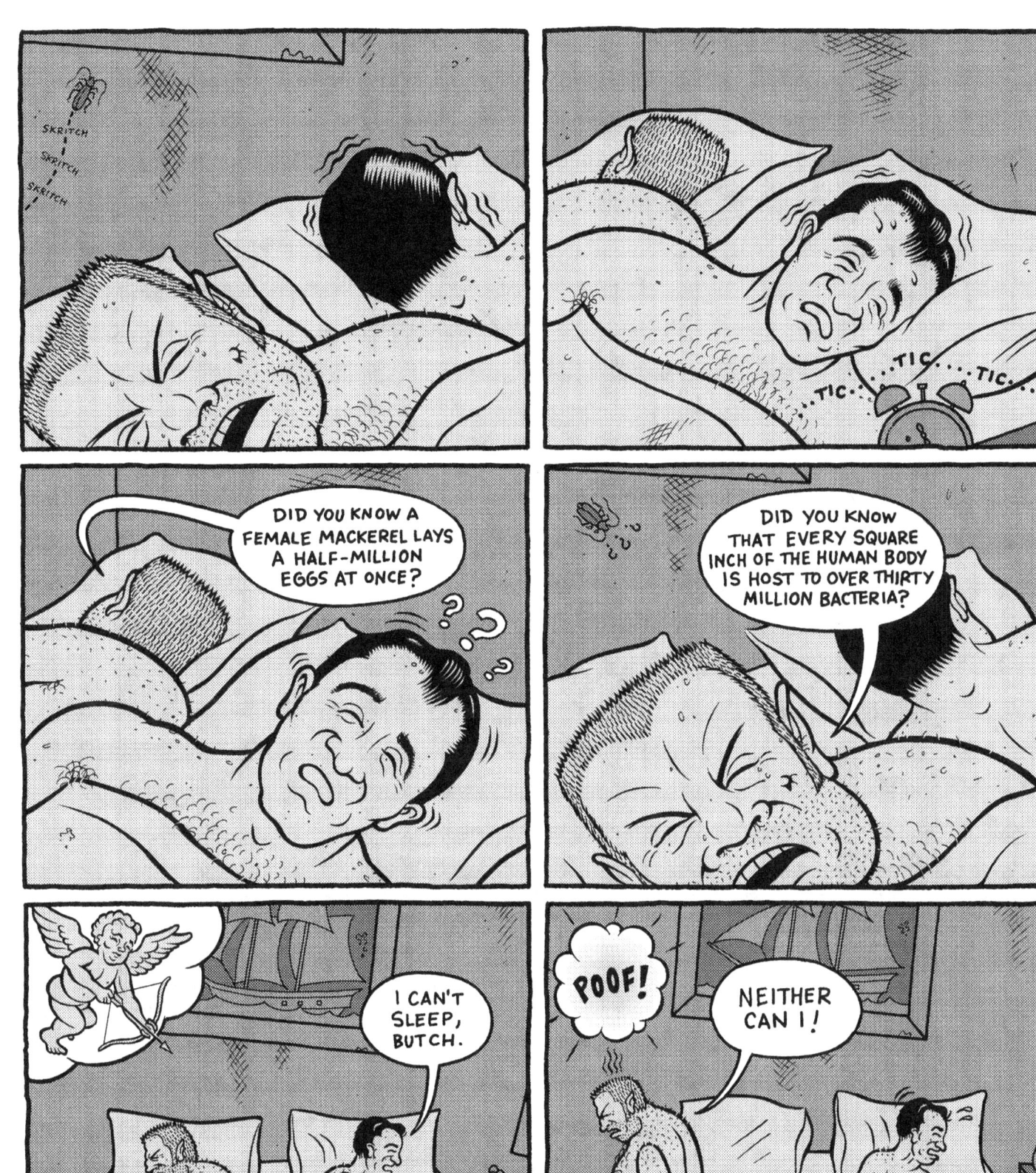

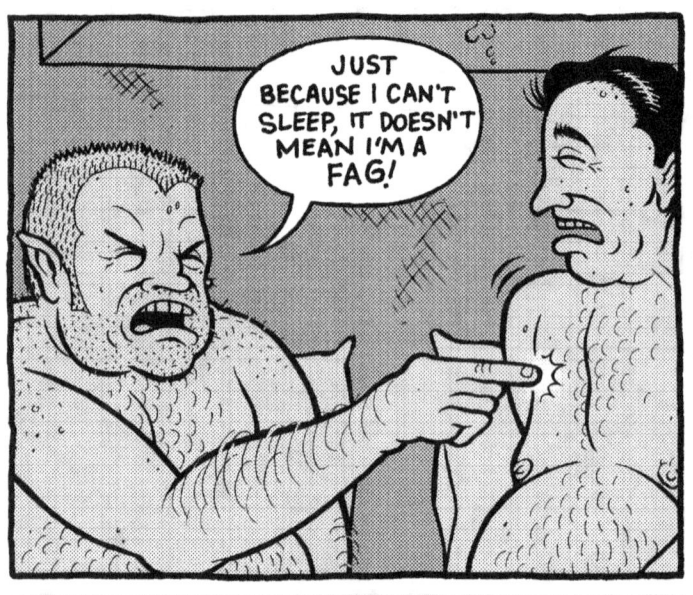

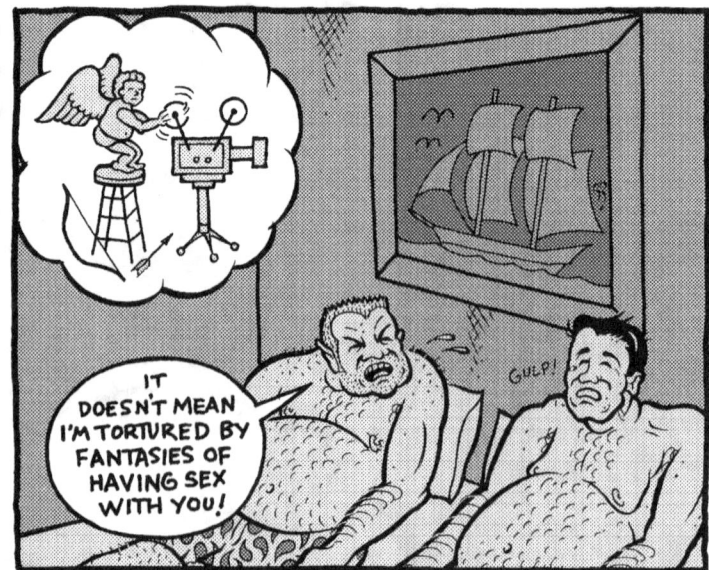

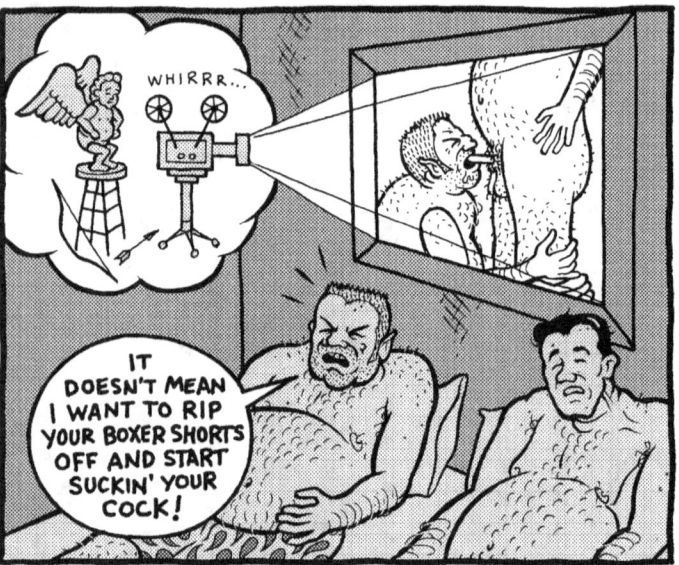

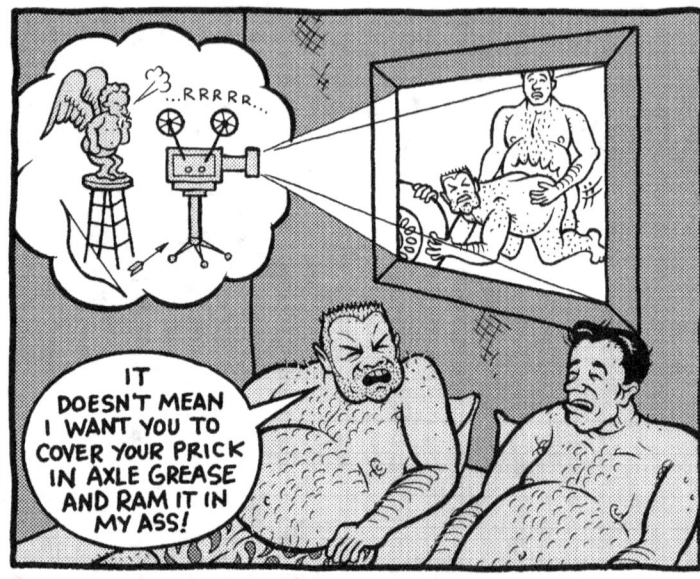

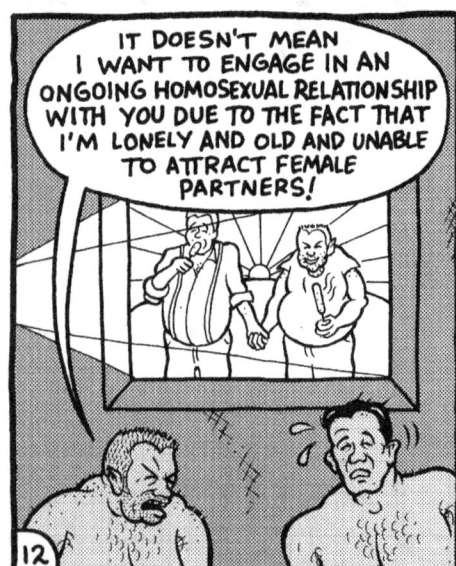

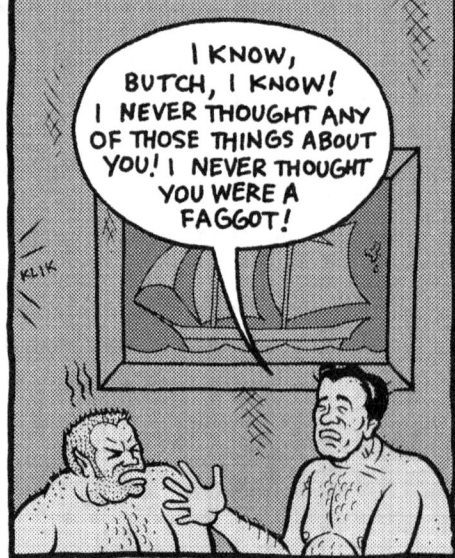

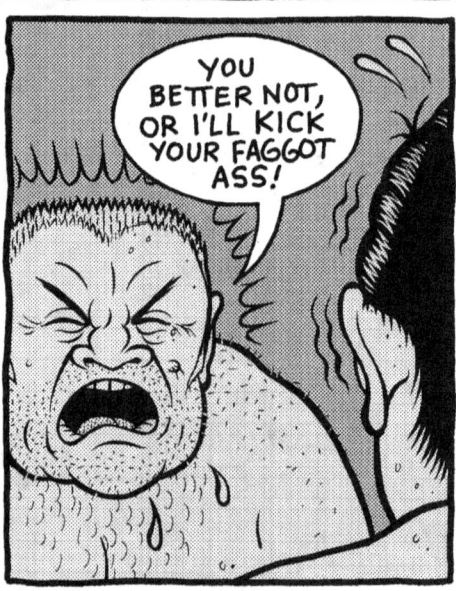

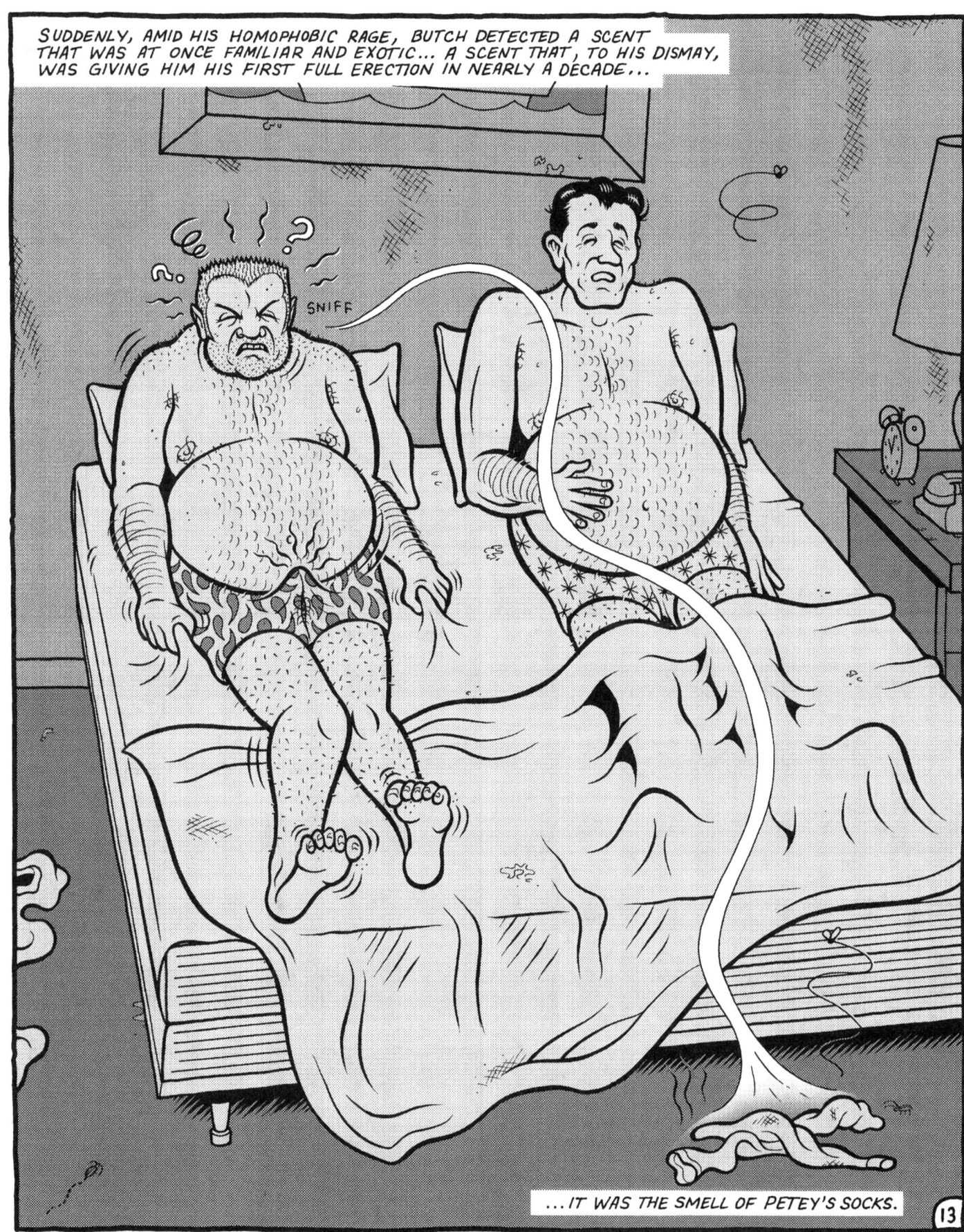

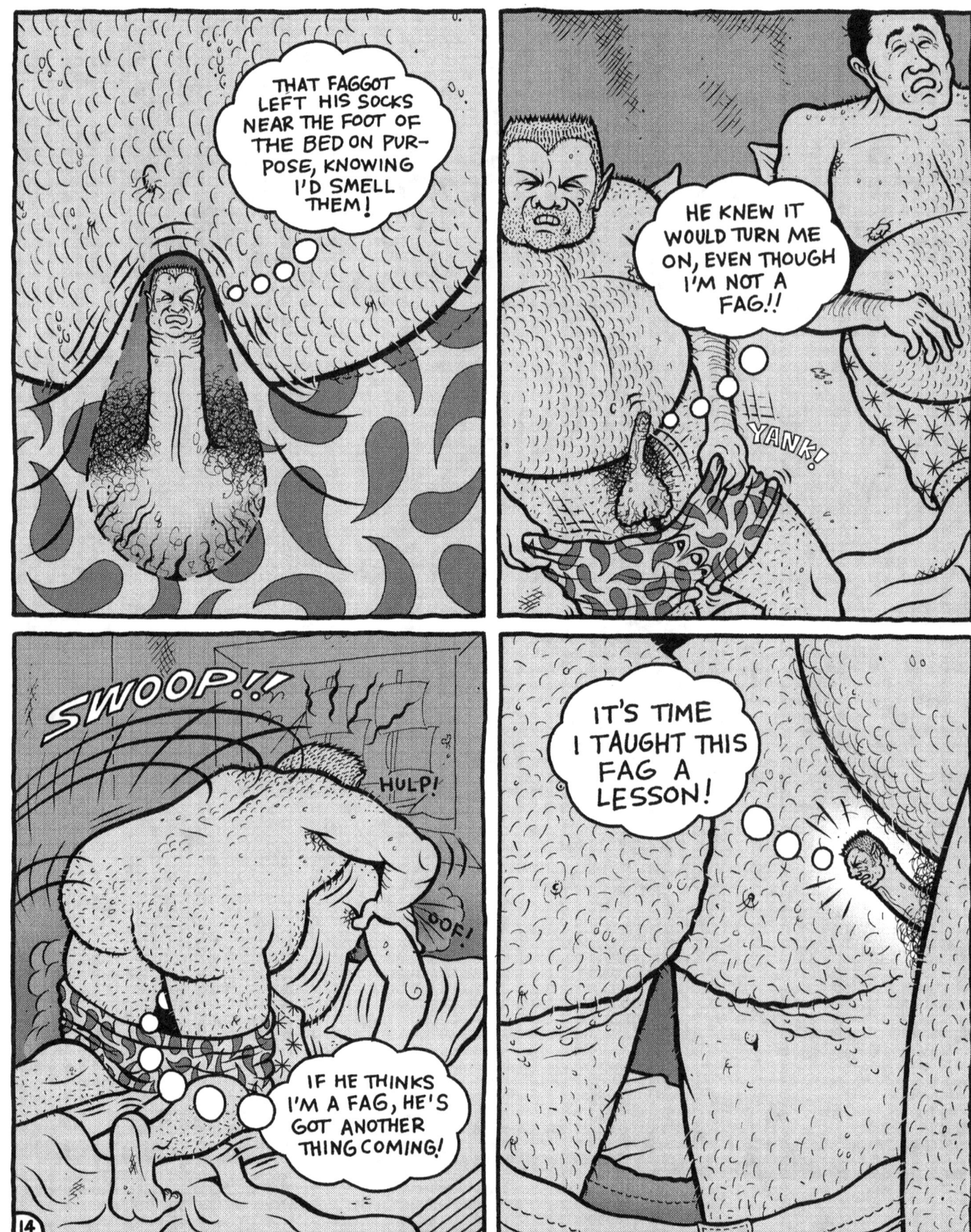

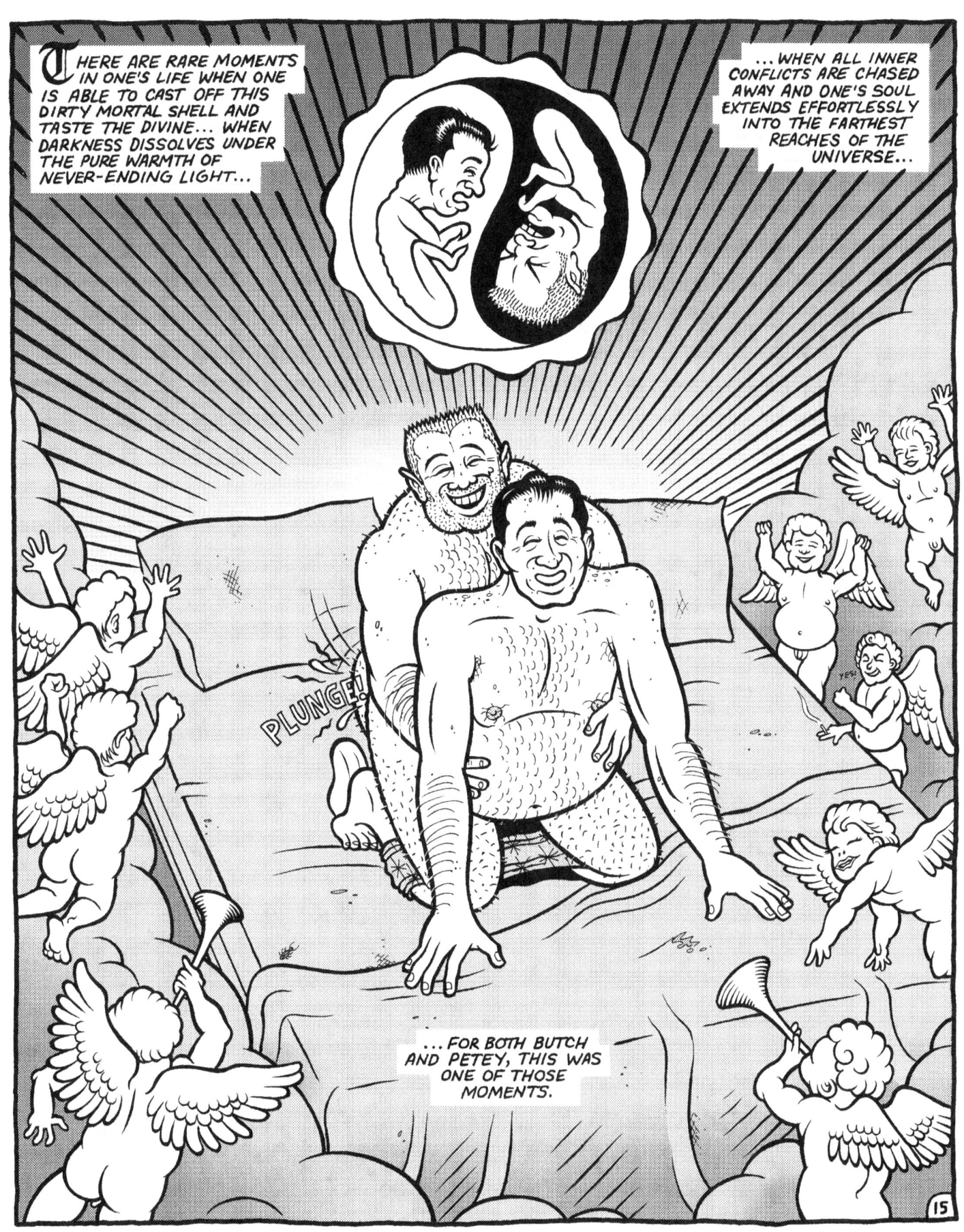

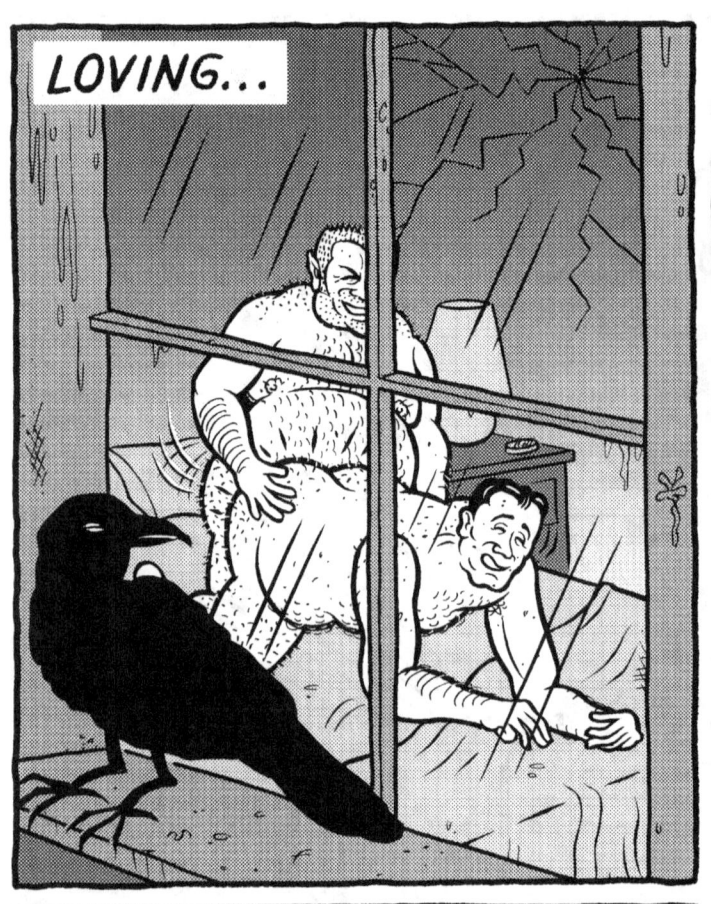

LOVING...

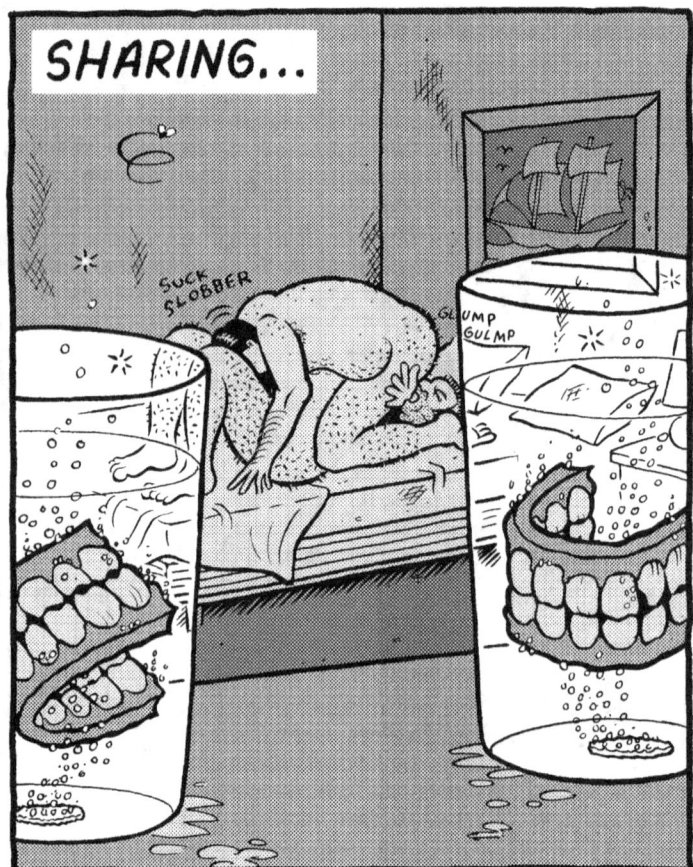

SHARING...

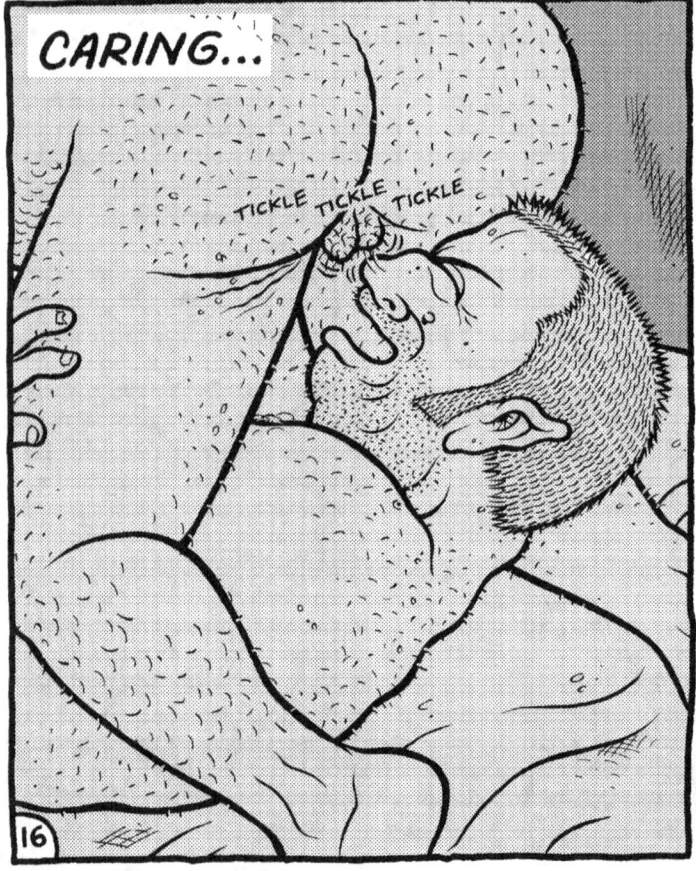

CARING...

16

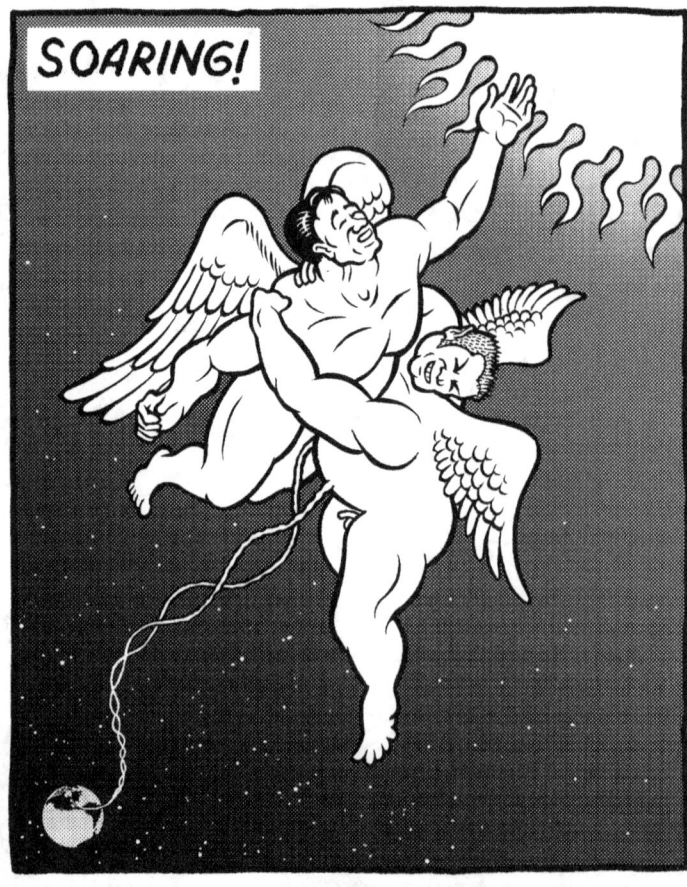

SOARING!

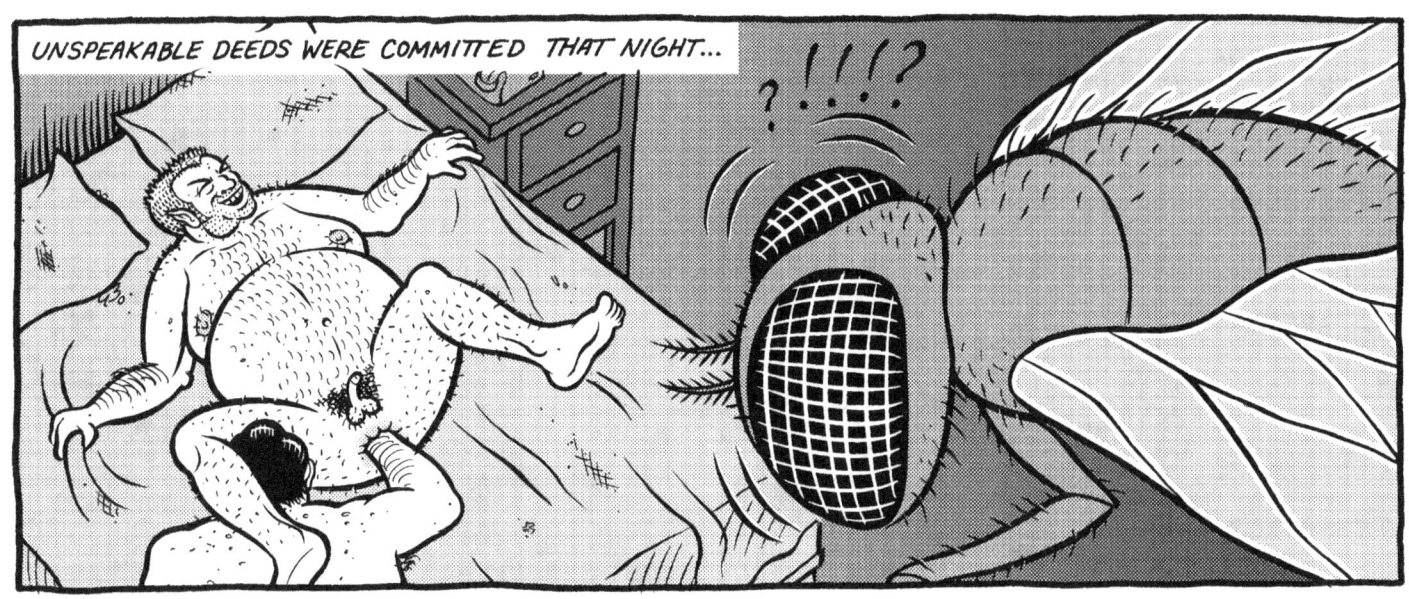

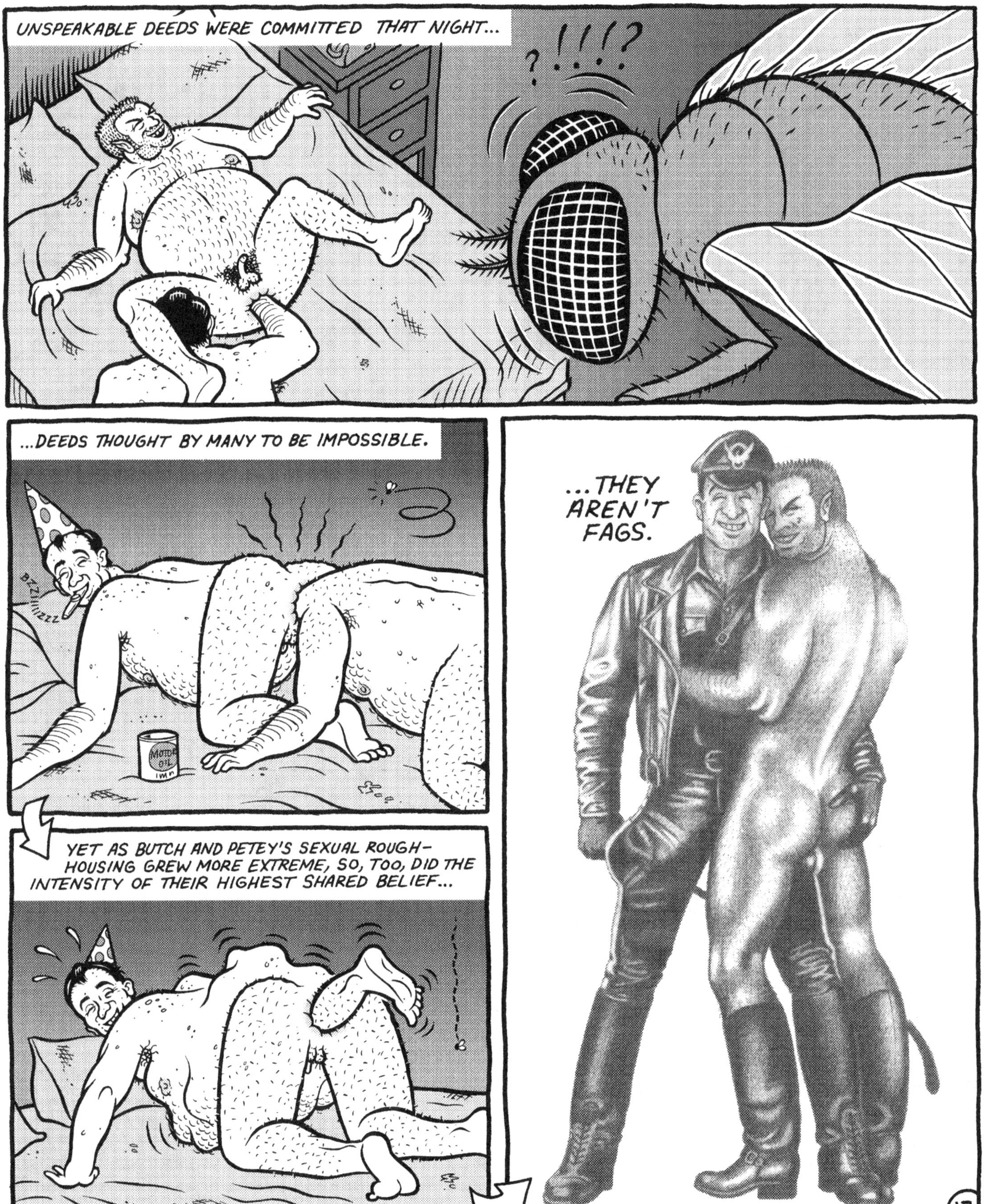

UNSPEAKABLE DEEDS WERE COMMITTED THAT NIGHT...

...DEEDS THOUGHT BY MANY TO BE IMPOSSIBLE.

YET AS BUTCH AND PETEY'S SEXUAL ROUGH-HOUSING GREW MORE EXTREME, SO, TOO, DID THE INTENSITY OF THEIR HIGHEST SHARED BELIEF...

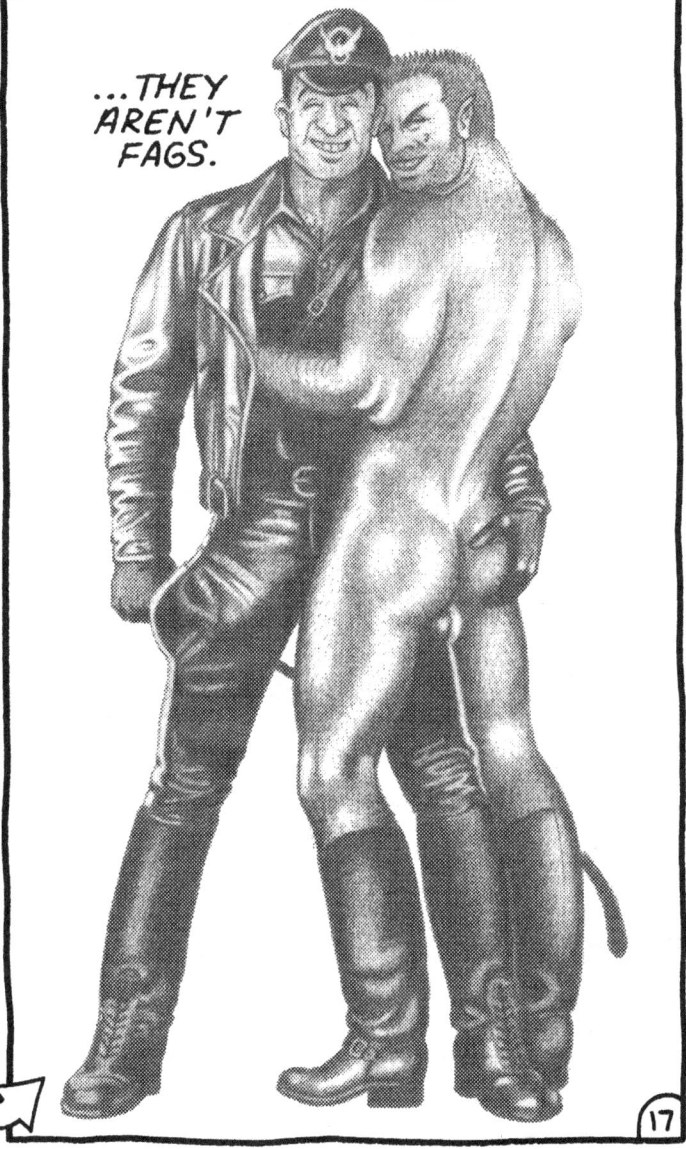

...THEY AREN'T FAGS.

17

AS DAYLIGHT SLOWLY FILLED THE MOTEL ROOM WITH THE FORCE OF TRUTH DISPELLING IGNORANCE...

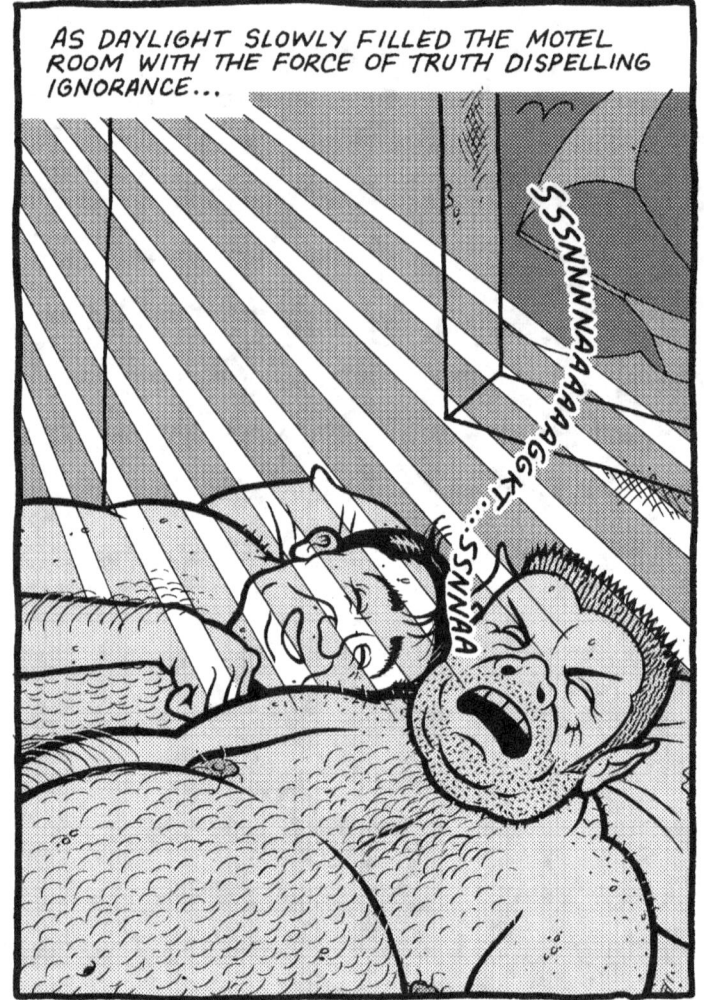

...AND THE PRIOR NIGHT'S ACTIVITIES BEGAN TO FLOOD THE BATTERED PSYCHES OF THESE SAD, AGING MEN...

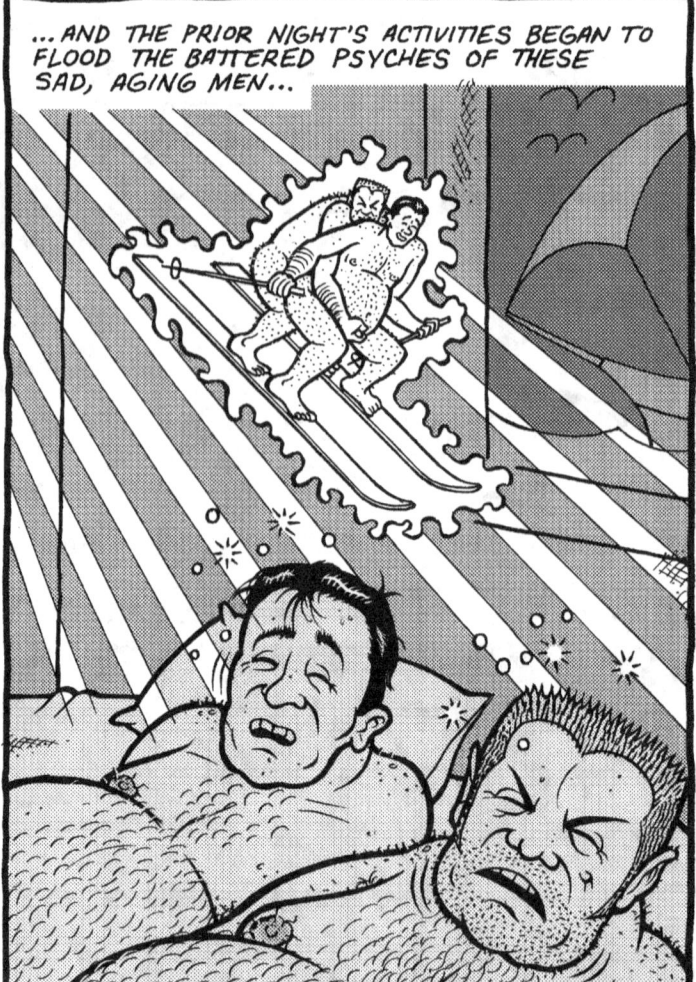

...BUTCH AND PETEY REALIZED THEY HAD A LOT OF EXPLAINING TO DO.

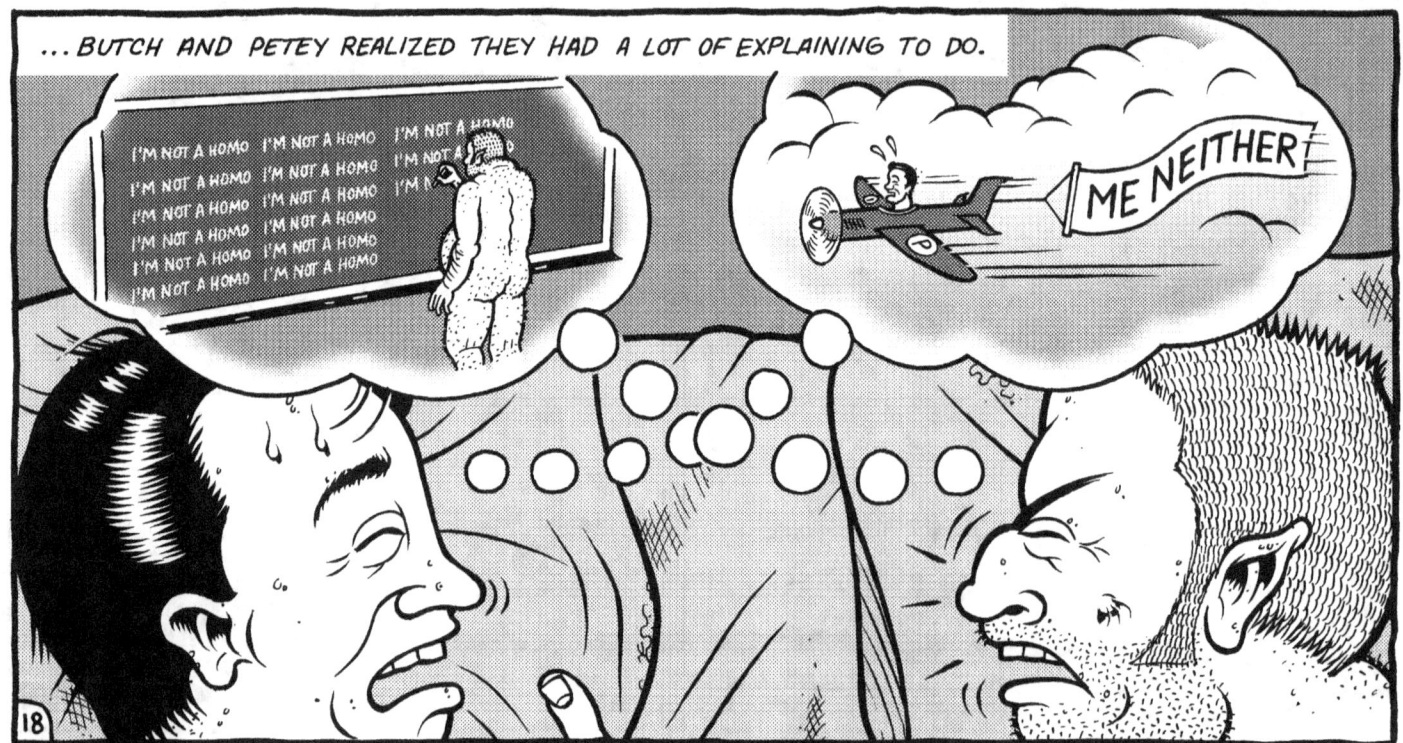

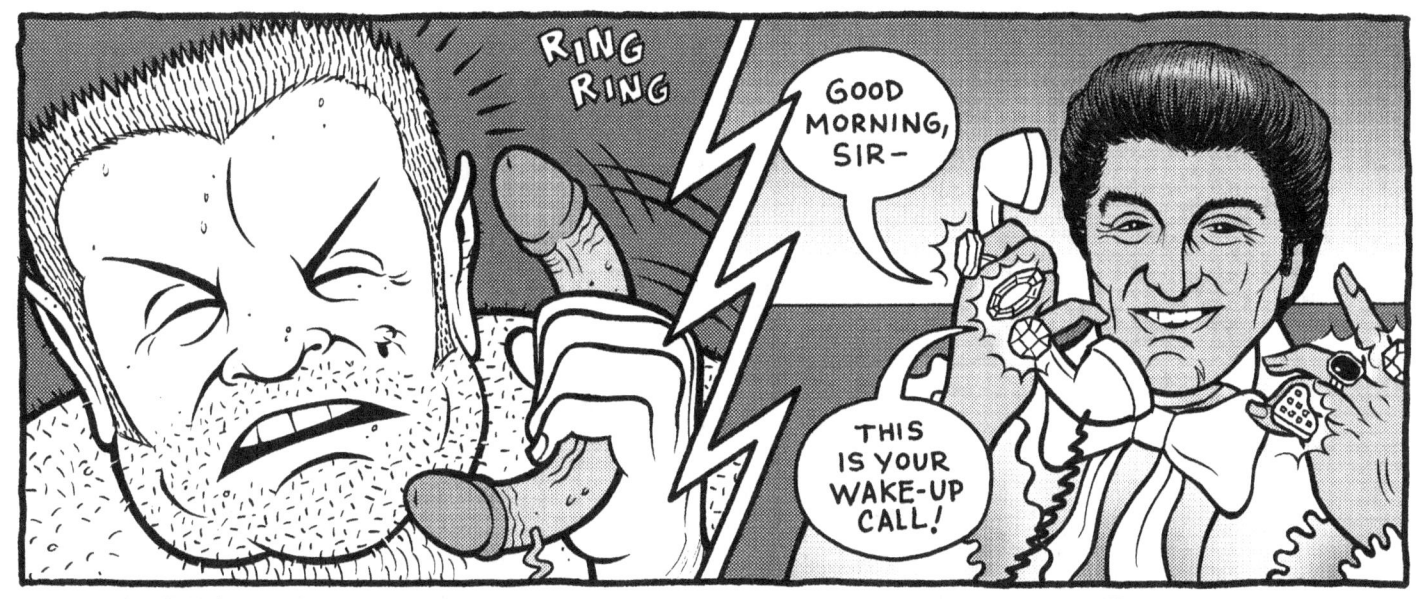

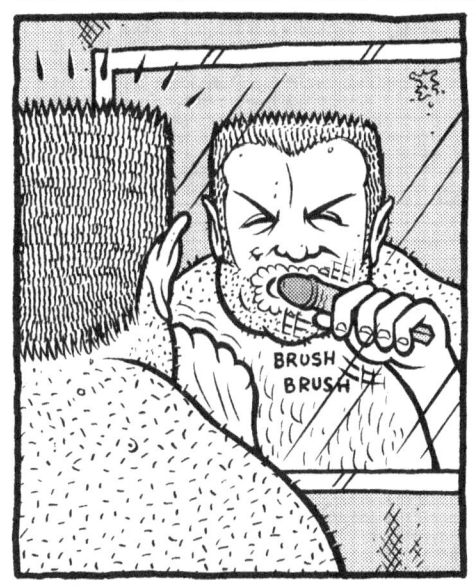

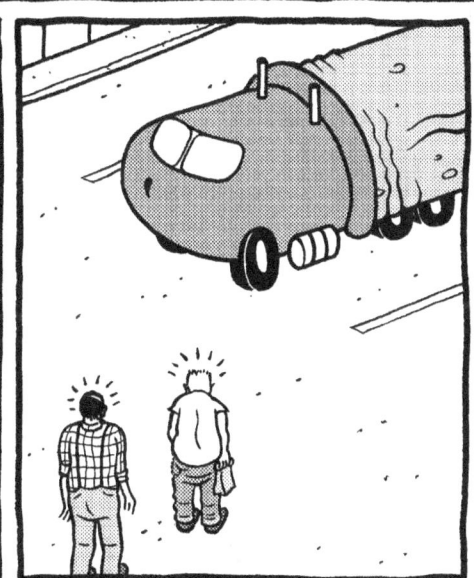

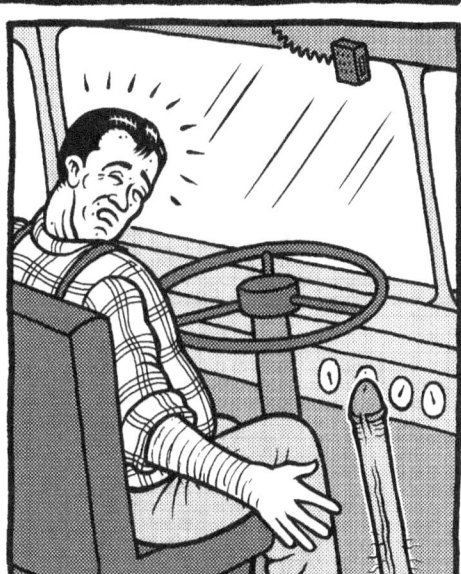

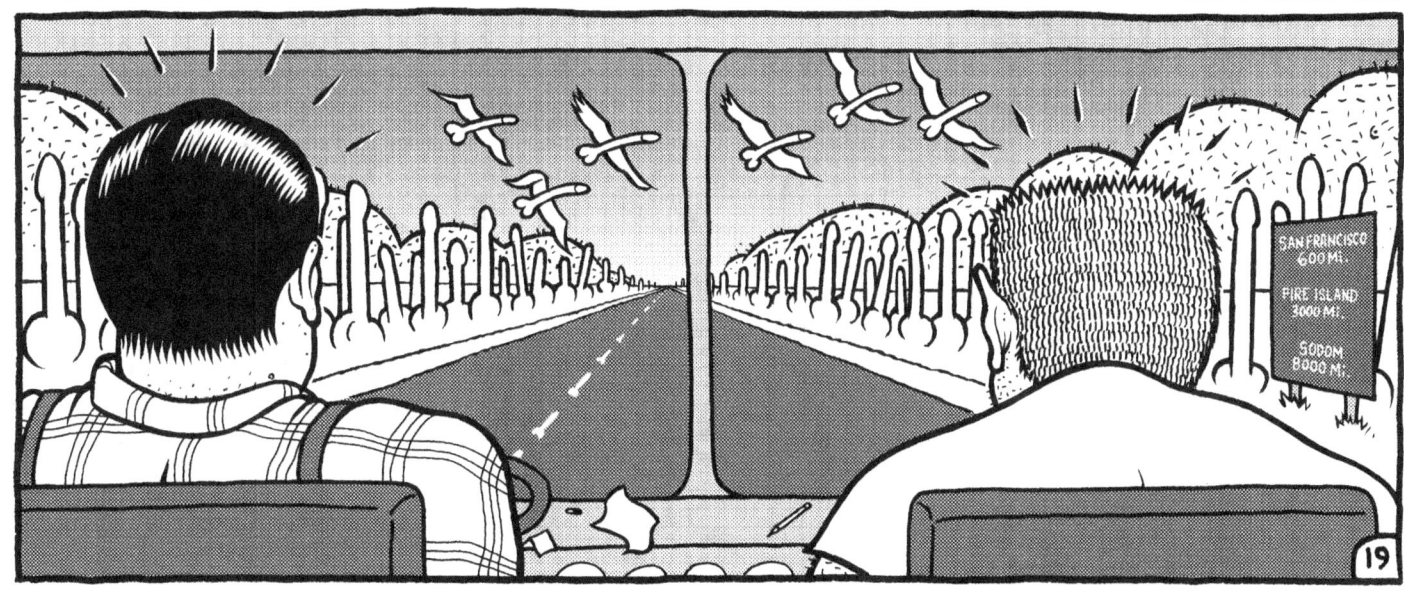

BUTCH AND PETEY'S WORKDAY PROCEEDED JUST AS IT HAD FOR YEARS: A TIGHT DEADLINE, A HEAVY LOAD, AND A THOUSAND MILES OF BAD ROAD.

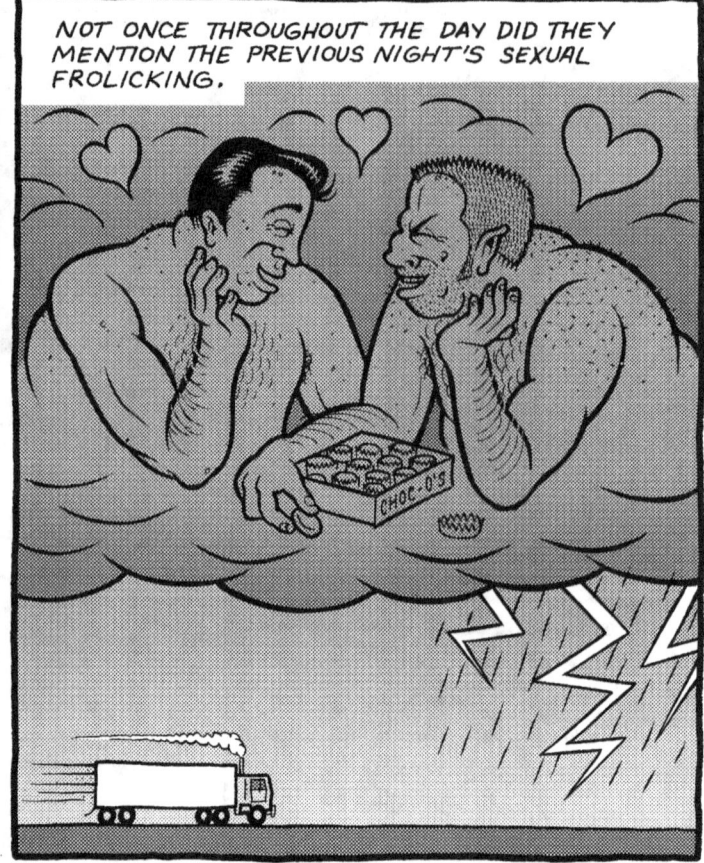

NOT ONCE THROUGHOUT THE DAY DID THEY MENTION THE PREVIOUS NIGHT'S SEXUAL FROLICKING.

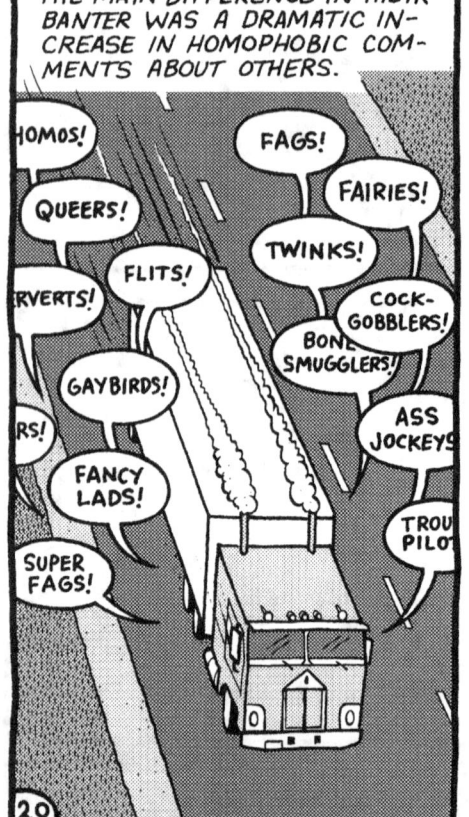

THE MAIN DIFFERENCE IN THEIR BANTER WAS A DRAMATIC INCREASE IN HOMOPHOBIC COMMENTS ABOUT OTHERS.

HOMOS!

QUEERS!

RVERTS!

FLITS!

GAYBIRDS!

RS!

FANCY LADS!

SUPER FAGS!

FAGS!

FAIRIES!

TWINKS!

COCK-GOBBLERS!

BONE SMUGGLERS!

ASS JOCKEYS!

TROU PILOT

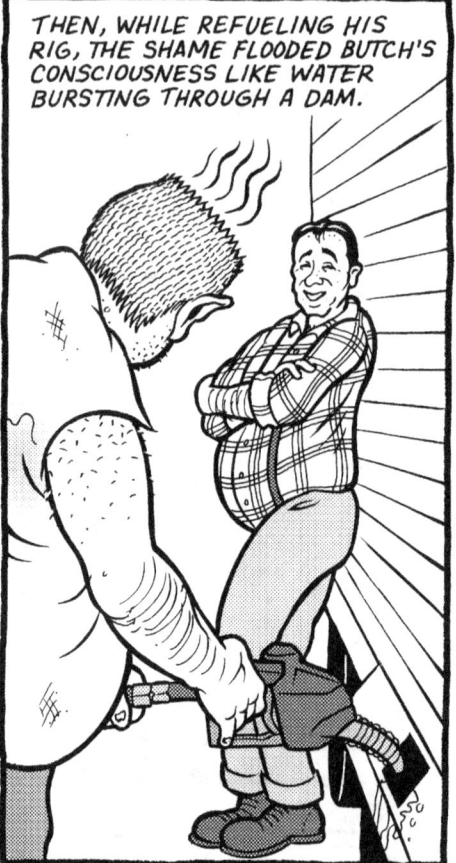

THEN, WHILE REFUELING HIS RIG, THE SHAME FLOODED BUTCH'S CONSCIOUSNESS LIKE WATER BURSTING THROUGH A DAM.

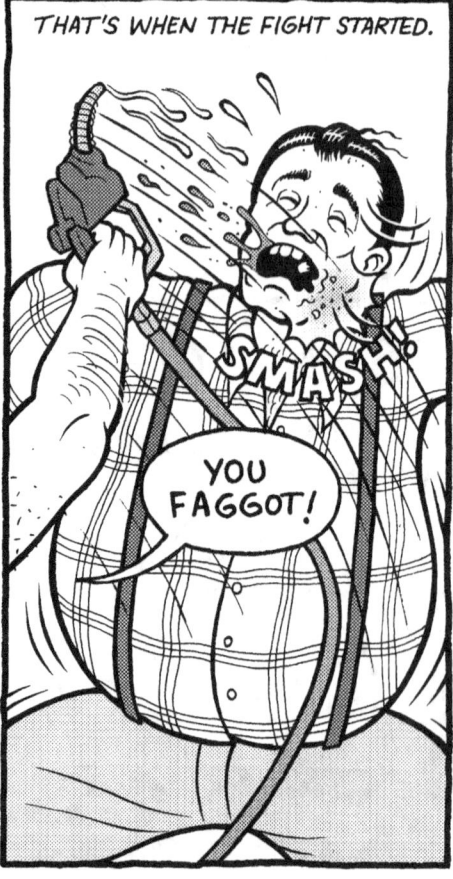

THAT'S WHEN THE FIGHT STARTED.

SMASH!

YOU FAGGOT!

MANY PSYCHOLOGISTS SPECULATE THAT EXCESSIVE VIOLENCE BETWEEN MEN IS A SIGN OF REPRESSED HOMOSEXUALITY.

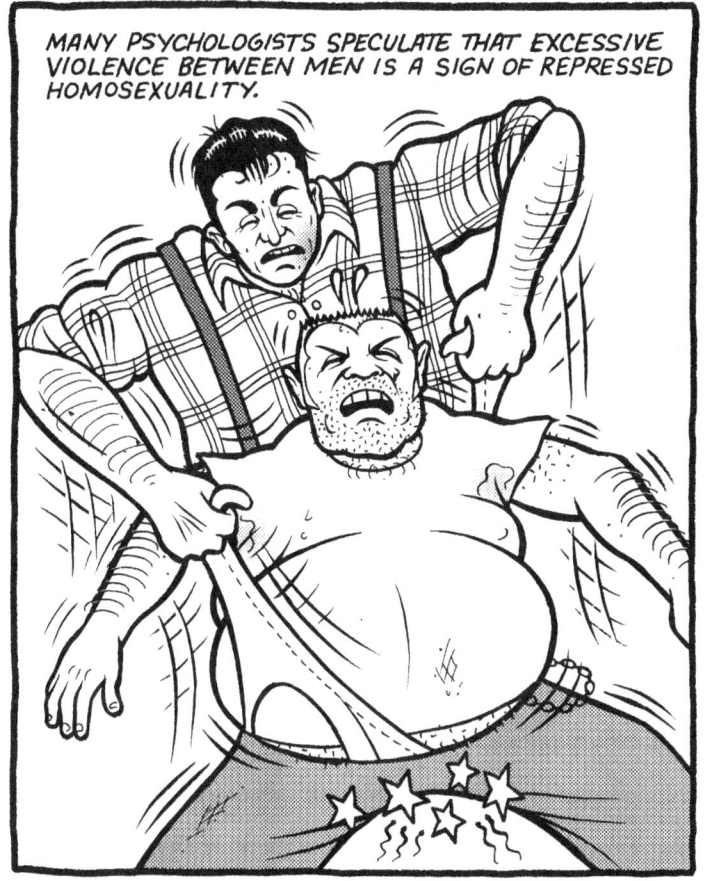

VIOLENCE ALLOWS MEN TO PASSIONATELY TOUCH ONE ANOTHER WITHOUT DIRECTLY ALLUDING TO SEXUAL CONTACT.

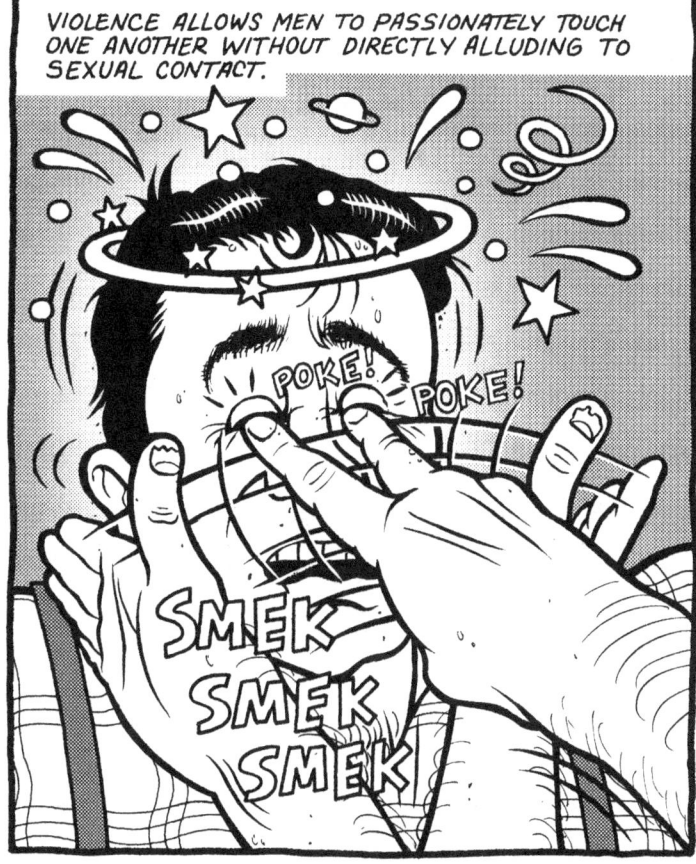

YET THERE REMAINS A CRUCIAL DISTINCTION BETWEEN VIOLENCE AND HOMOSEXUALITY.

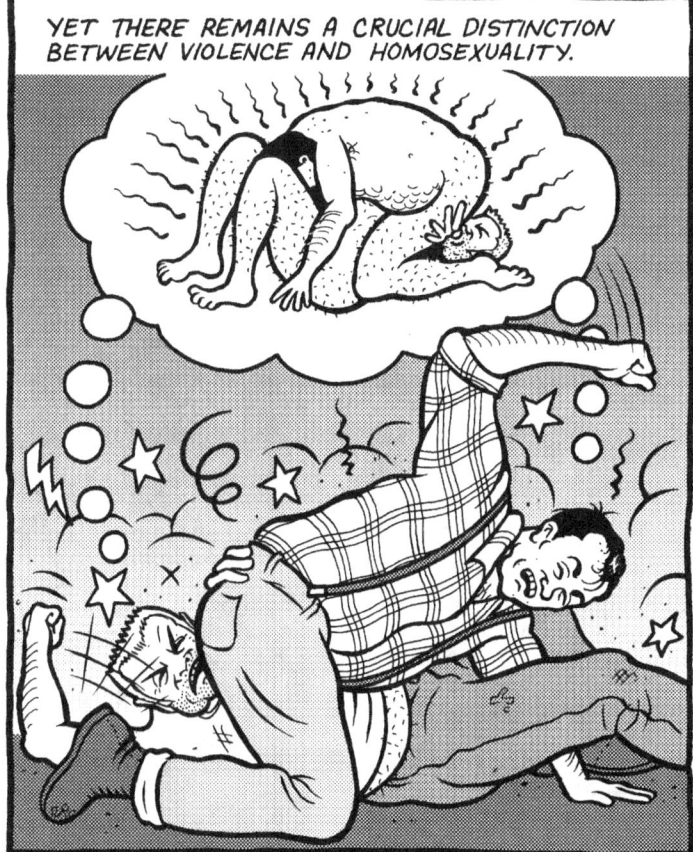

VIOLENCE IS ILLEGAL.

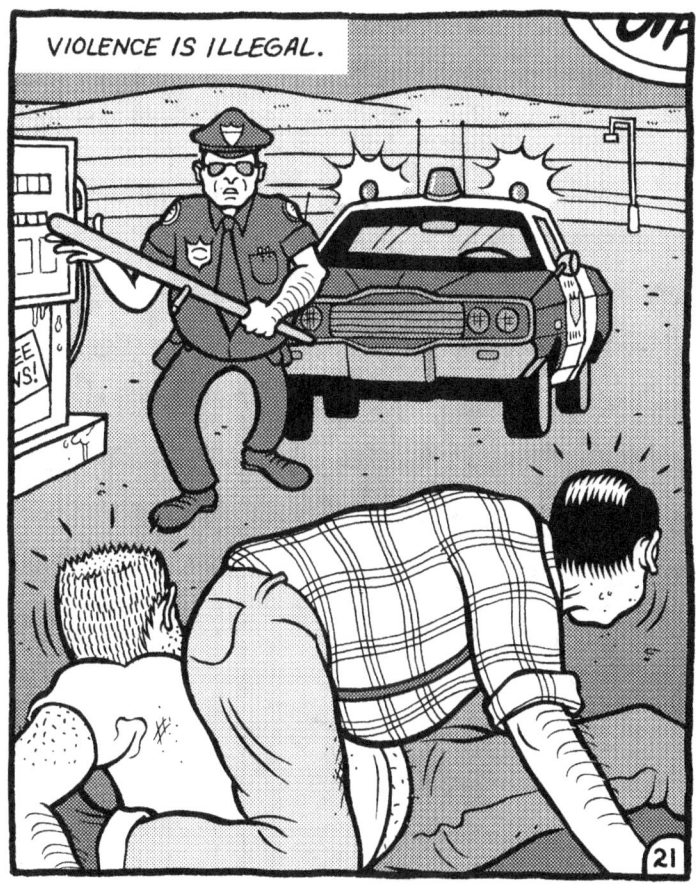

21

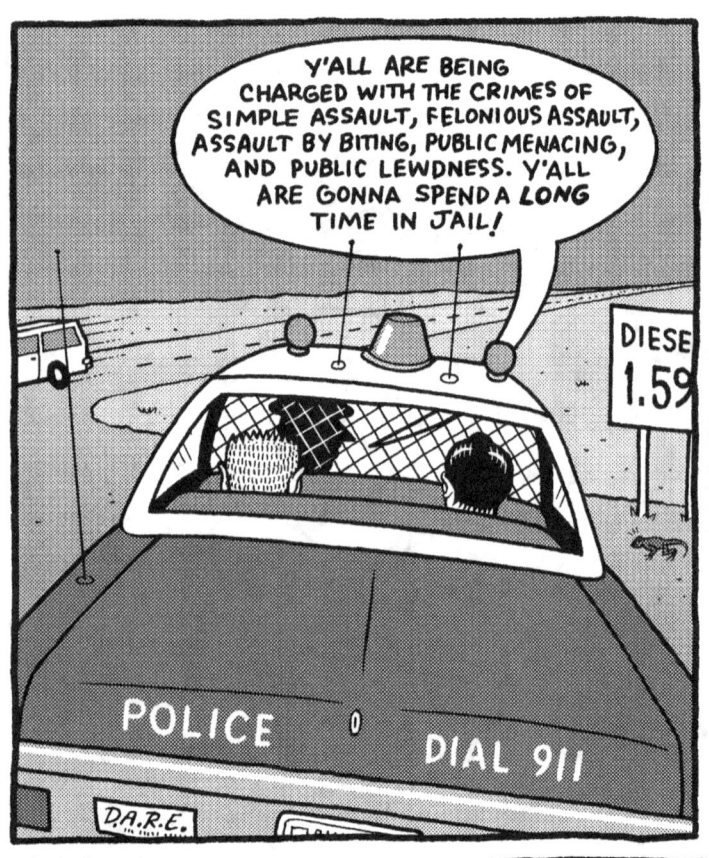

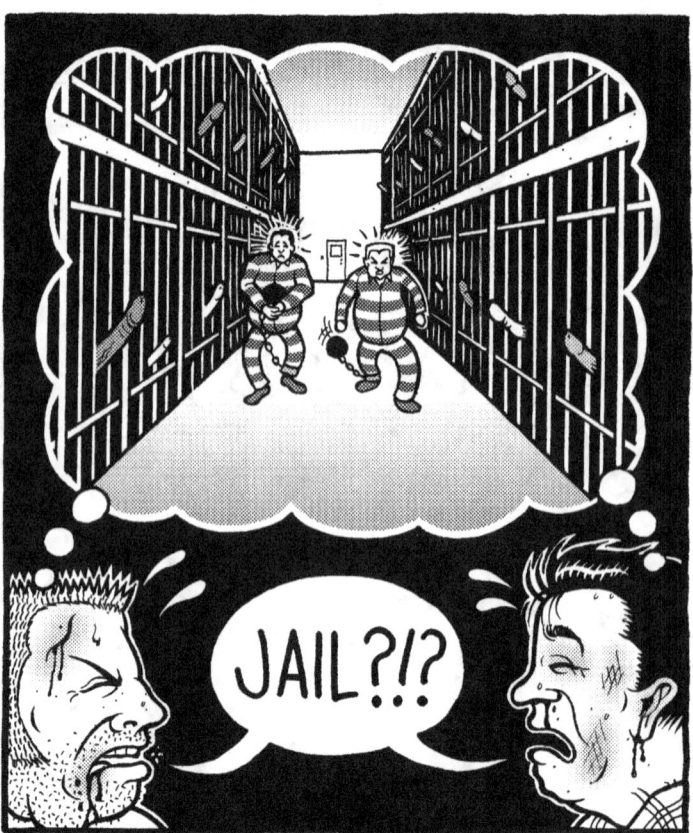

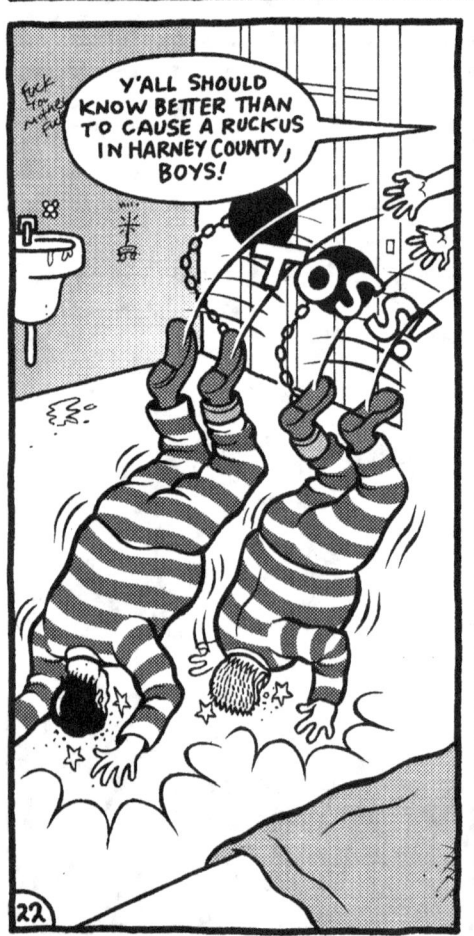

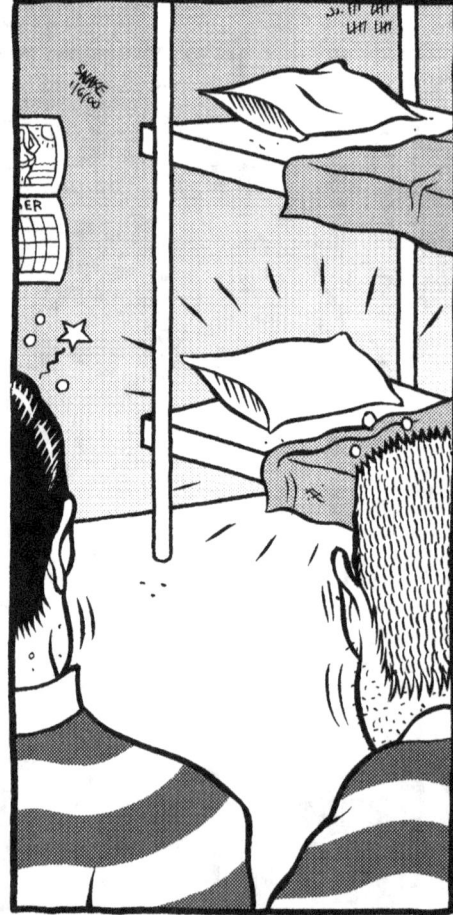

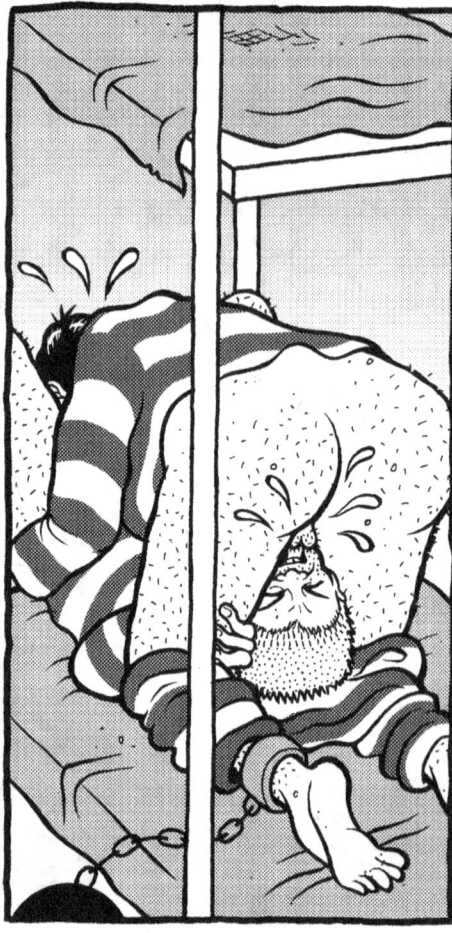

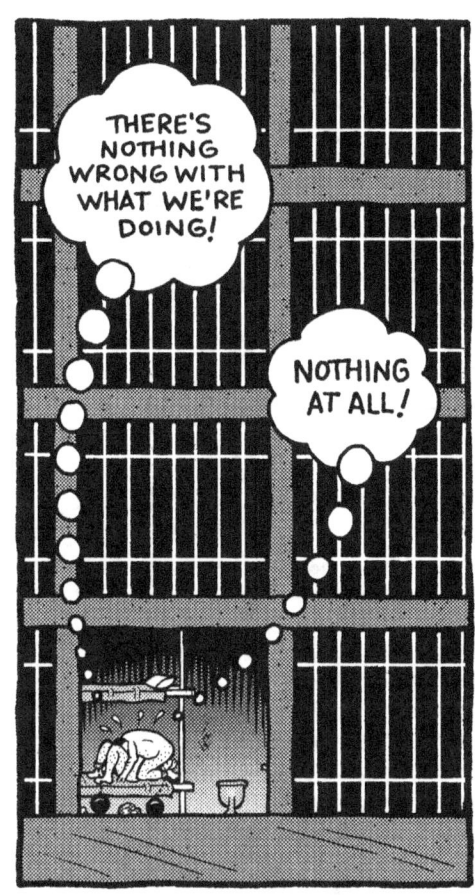

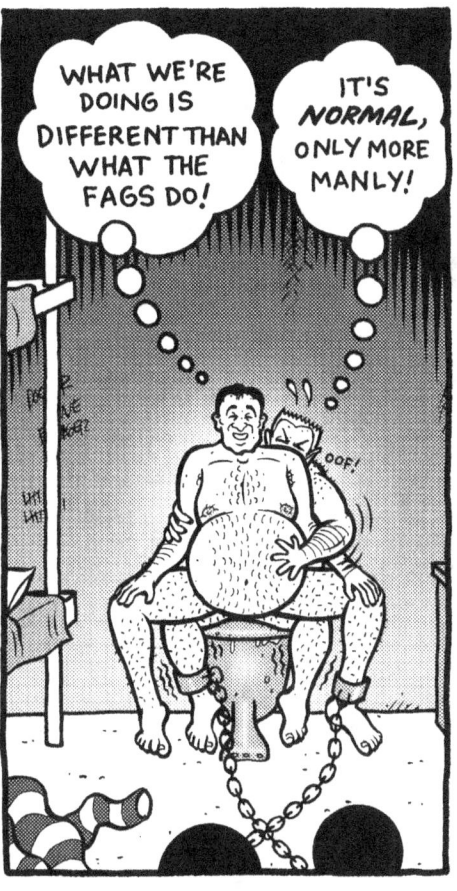

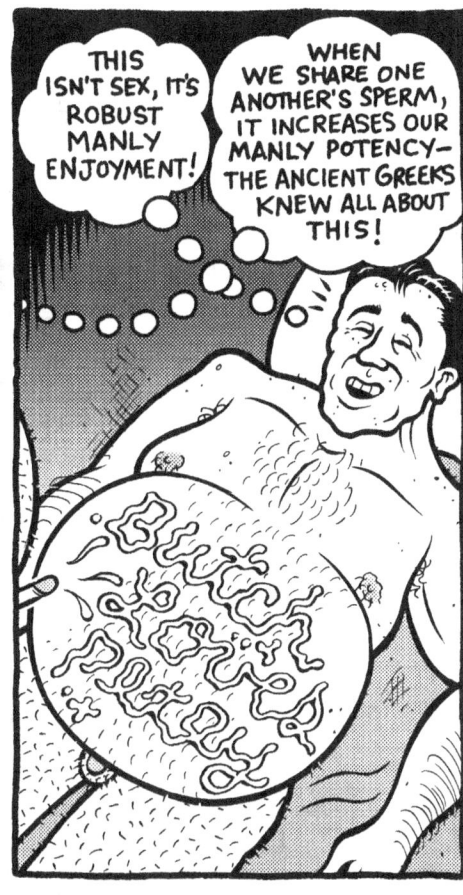

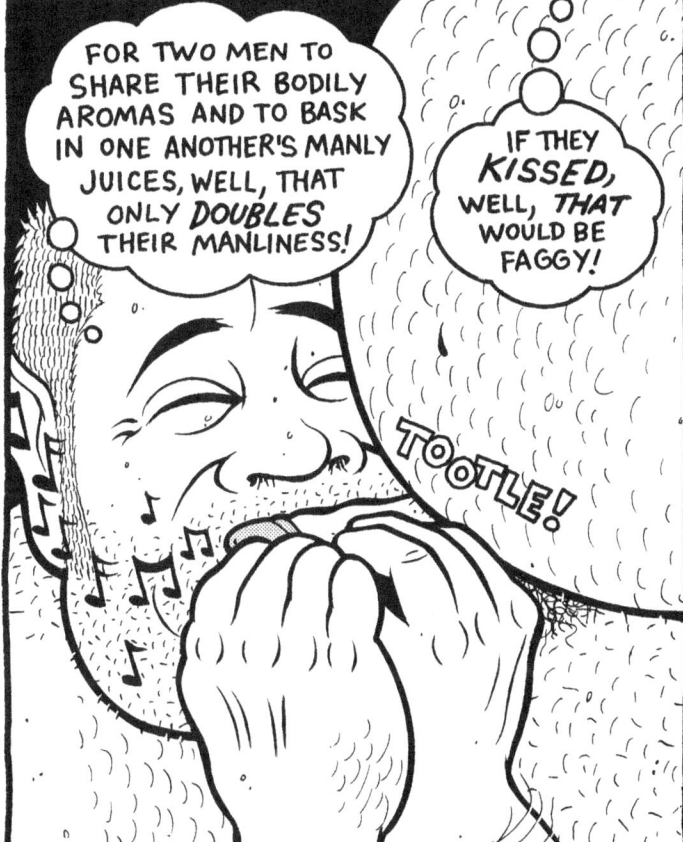

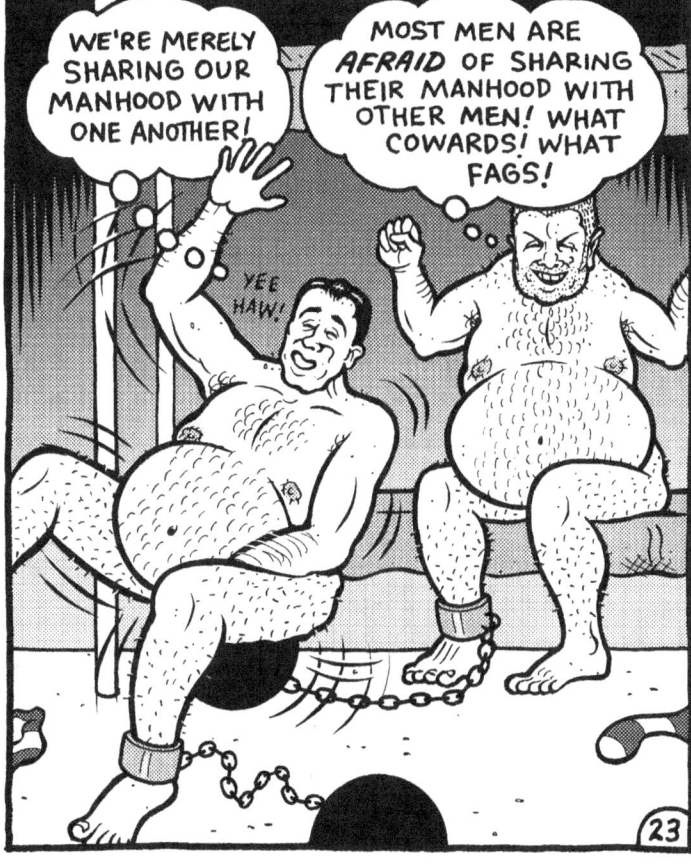

23

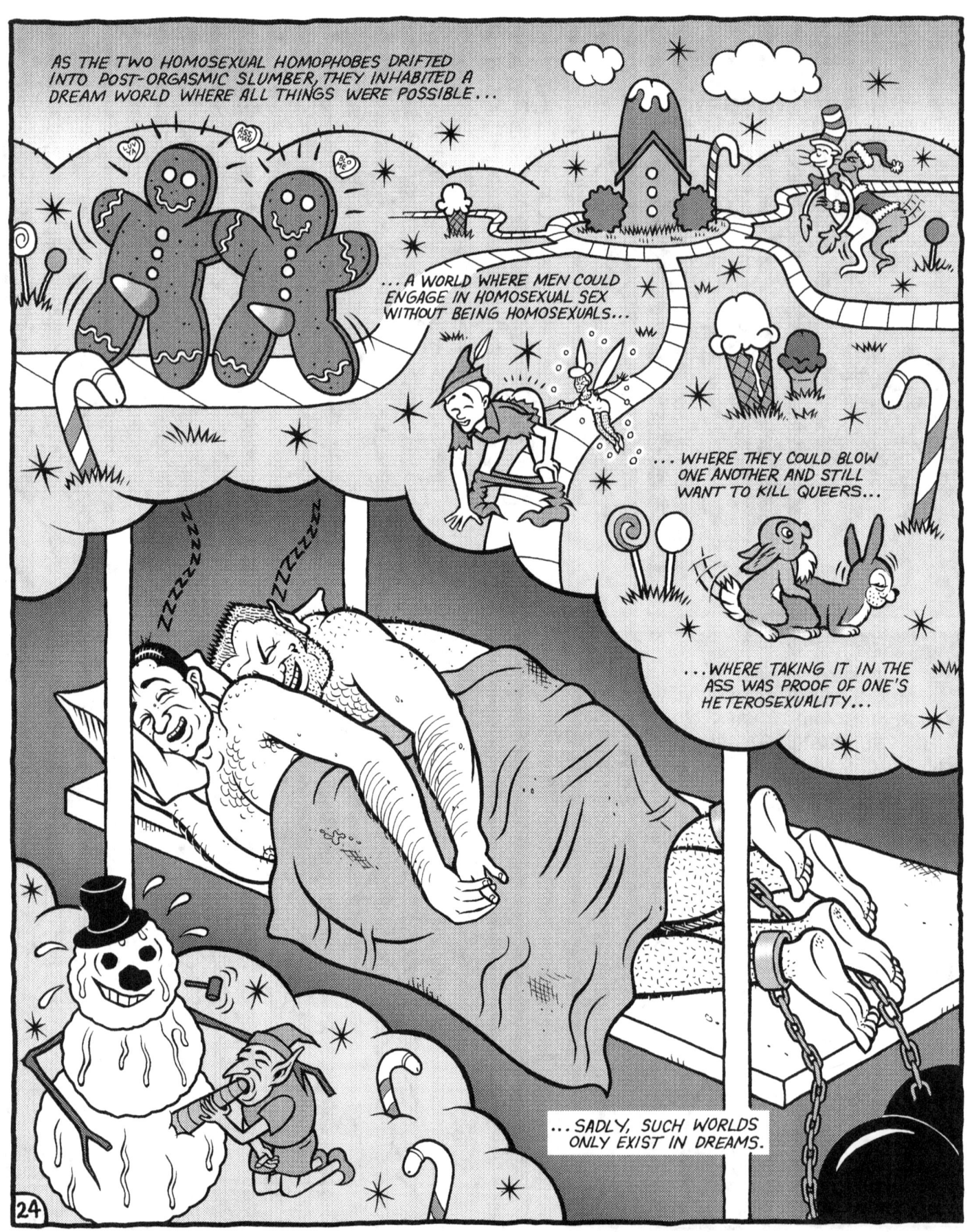

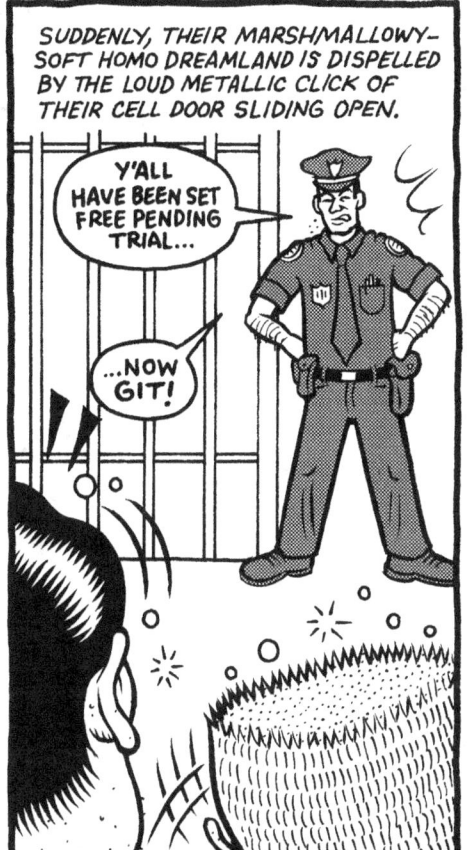

SUDDENLY, THEIR MARSHMALLOWY-SOFT HOMO DREAMLAND IS DISPELLED BY THE LOUD METALLIC CLICK OF THEIR CELL DOOR SLIDING OPEN.

Y'ALL HAVE BEEN SET FREE PENDING TRIAL...

...NOW GIT!

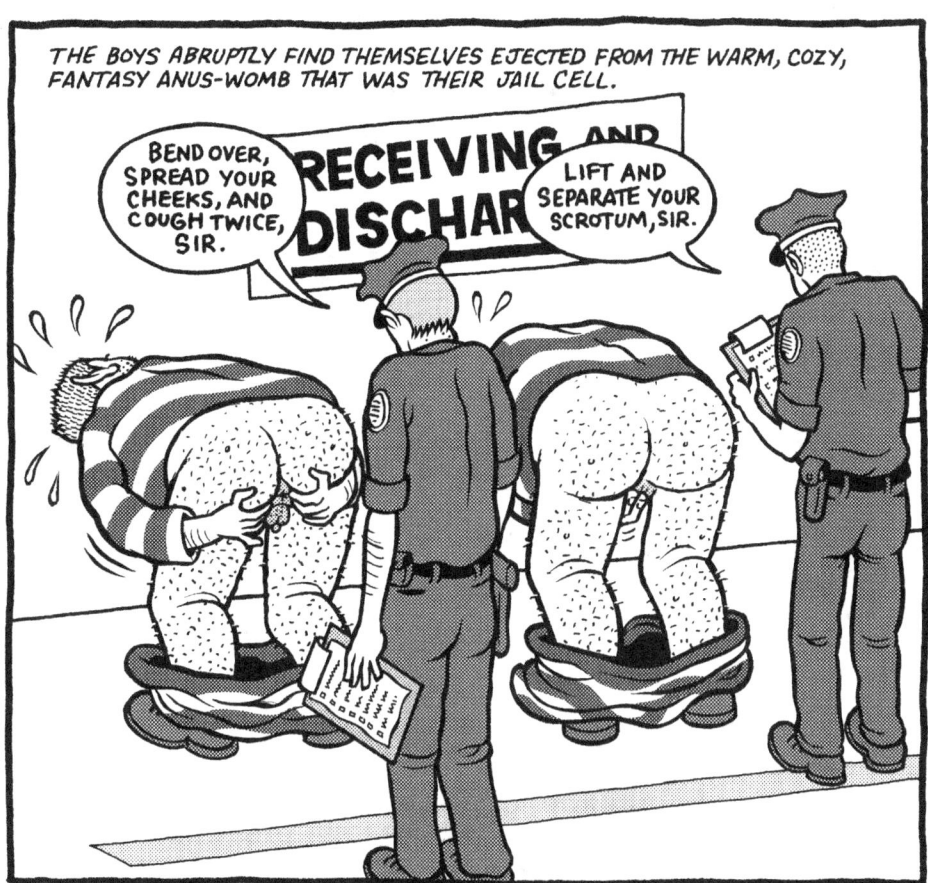

THE BOYS ABRUPTLY FIND THEMSELVES EJECTED FROM THE WARM, COZY, FANTASY ANUS-WOMB THAT WAS THEIR JAIL CELL.

BEND OVER, SPREAD YOUR CHEEKS, AND COUGH TWICE, SIR.

RECEIVING AND DISCHAR...

LIFT AND SEPARATE YOUR SCROTUM, SIR.

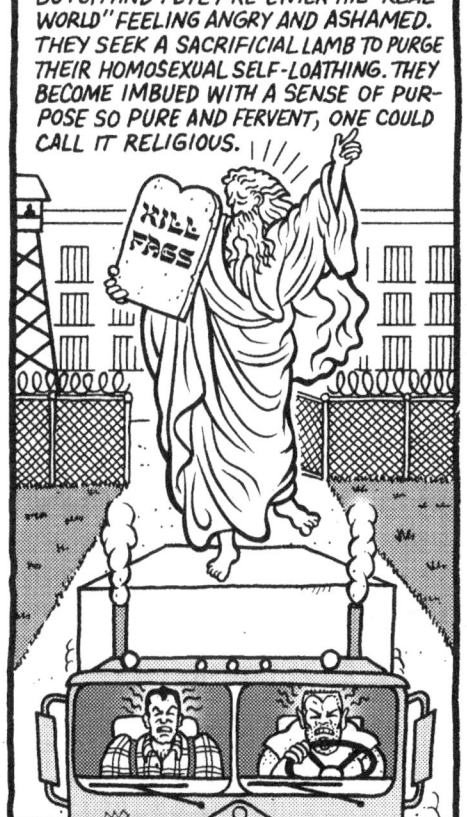

BUTCH AND PETEY RE-ENTER THE "REAL WORLD" FEELING ANGRY AND ASHAMED. THEY SEEK A SACRIFICIAL LAMB TO PURGE THEIR HOMOSEXUAL SELF-LOATHING. THEY BECOME IMBUED WITH A SENSE OF PUR-POSE SO PURE AND FERVENT, ONE COULD CALL IT RELIGIOUS.

KILL FAGS

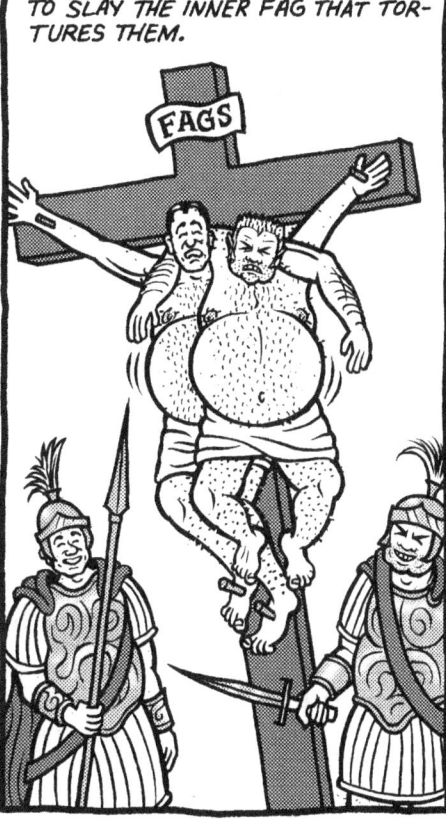

THEY KNOW THERE IS ONLY ONE WAY TO SLAY THE INNER FAG THAT TOR-TURES THEM.

FAGS

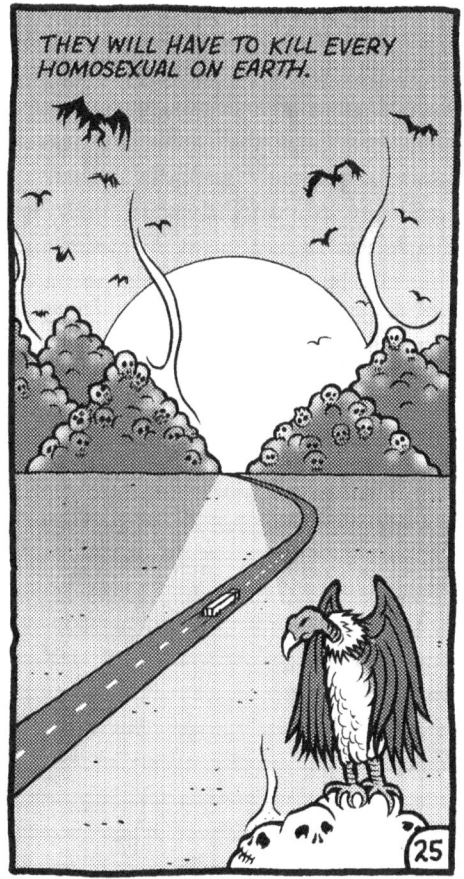

THEY WILL HAVE TO KILL EVERY HOMOSEXUAL ON EARTH.

25

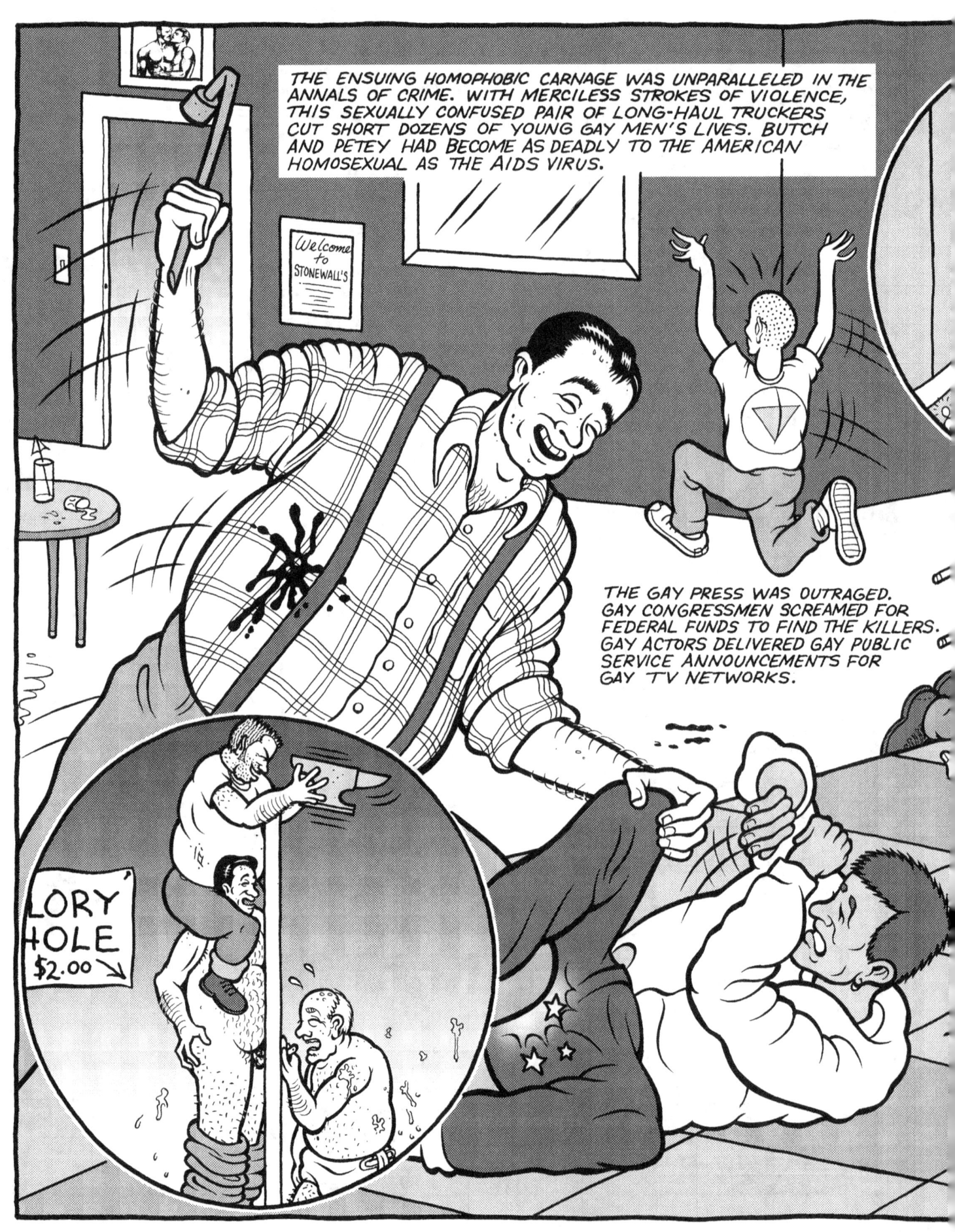

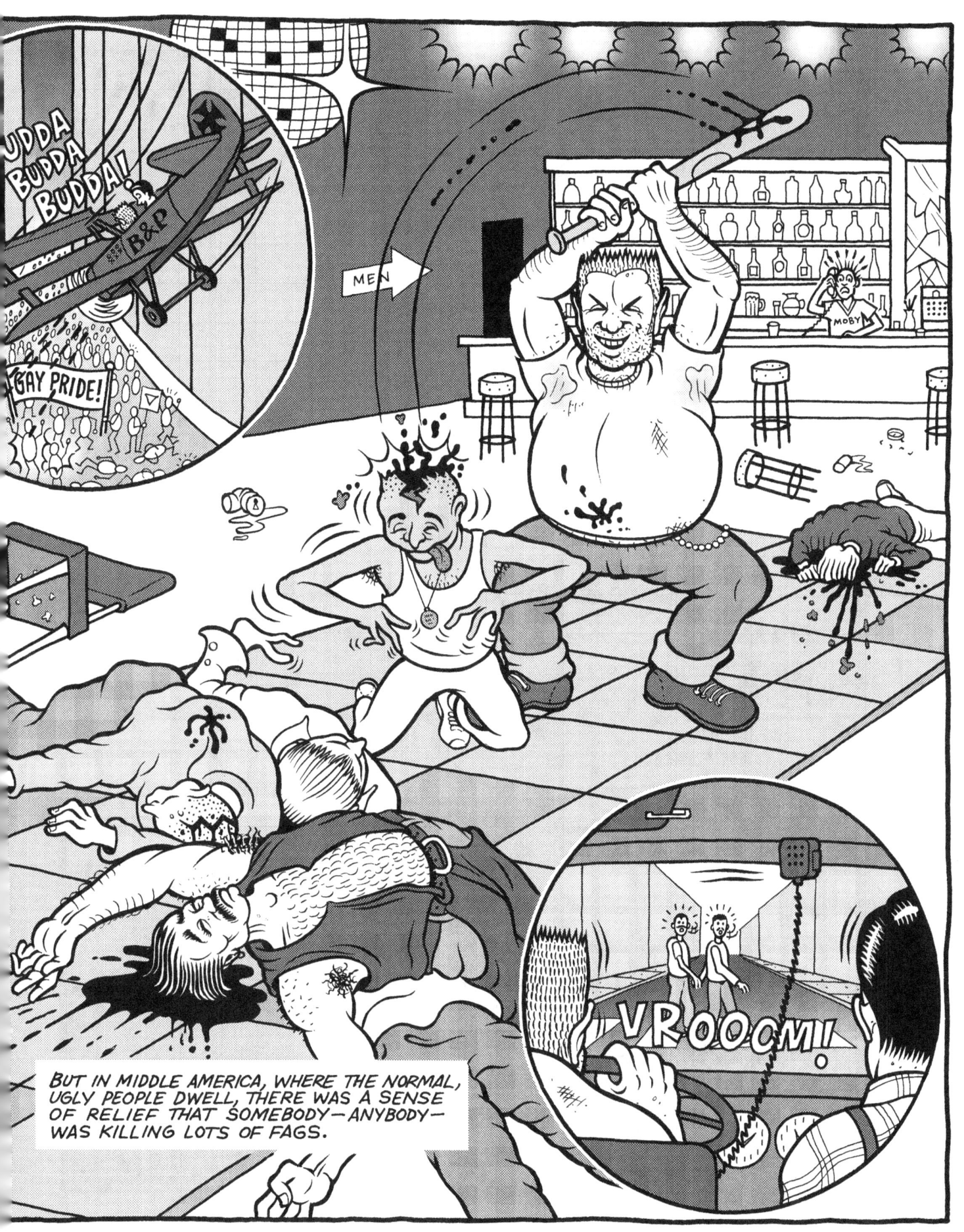

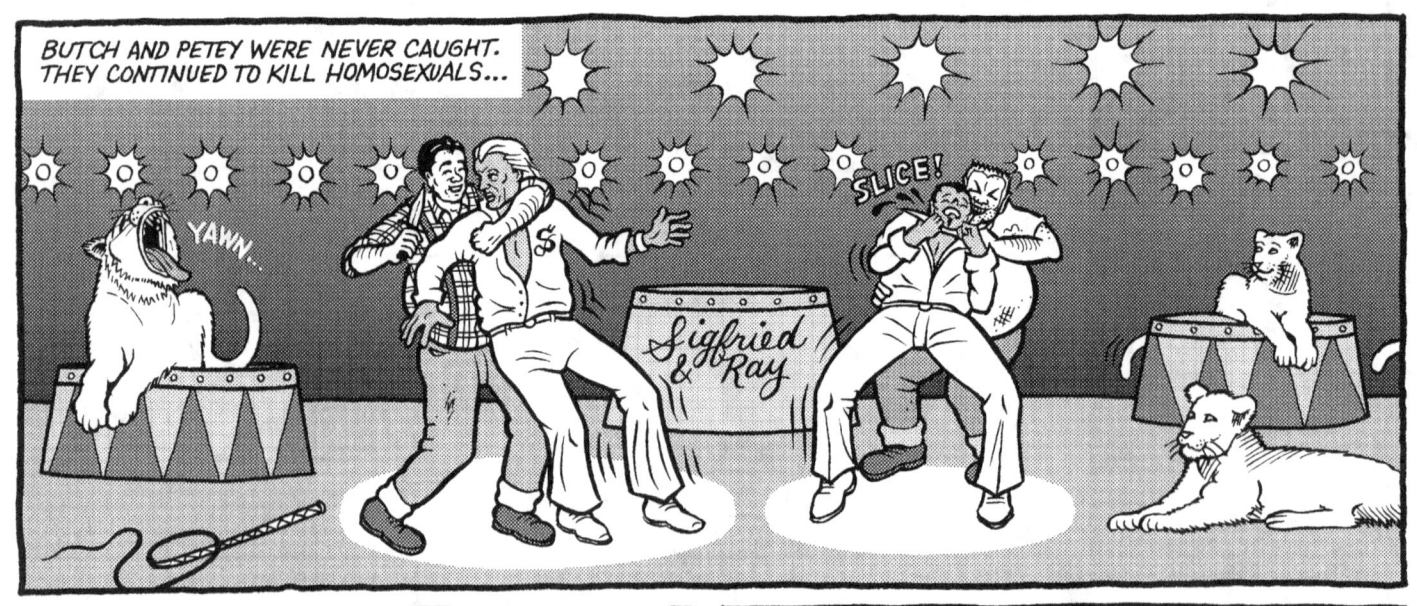

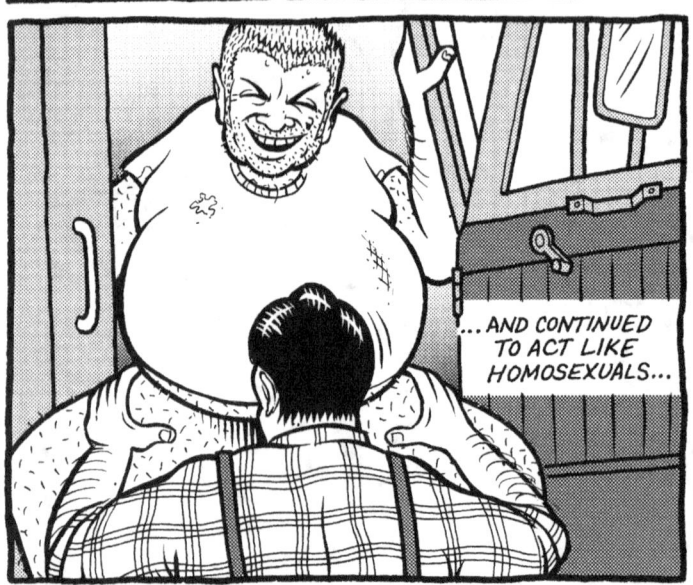

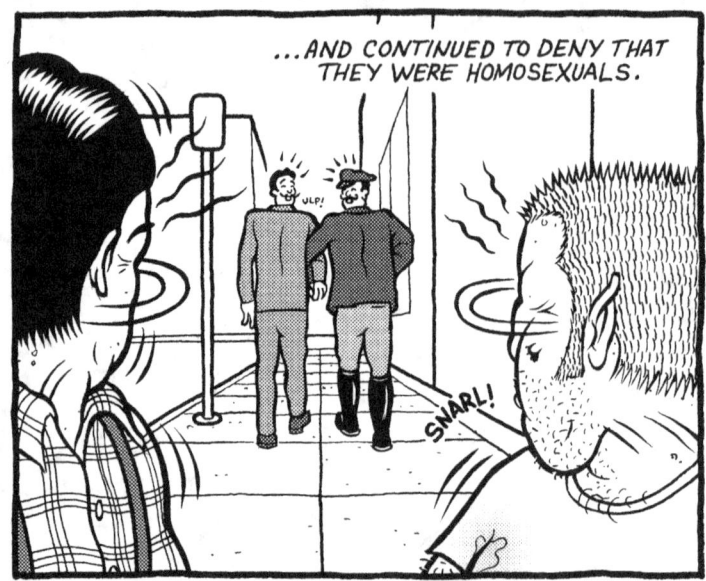

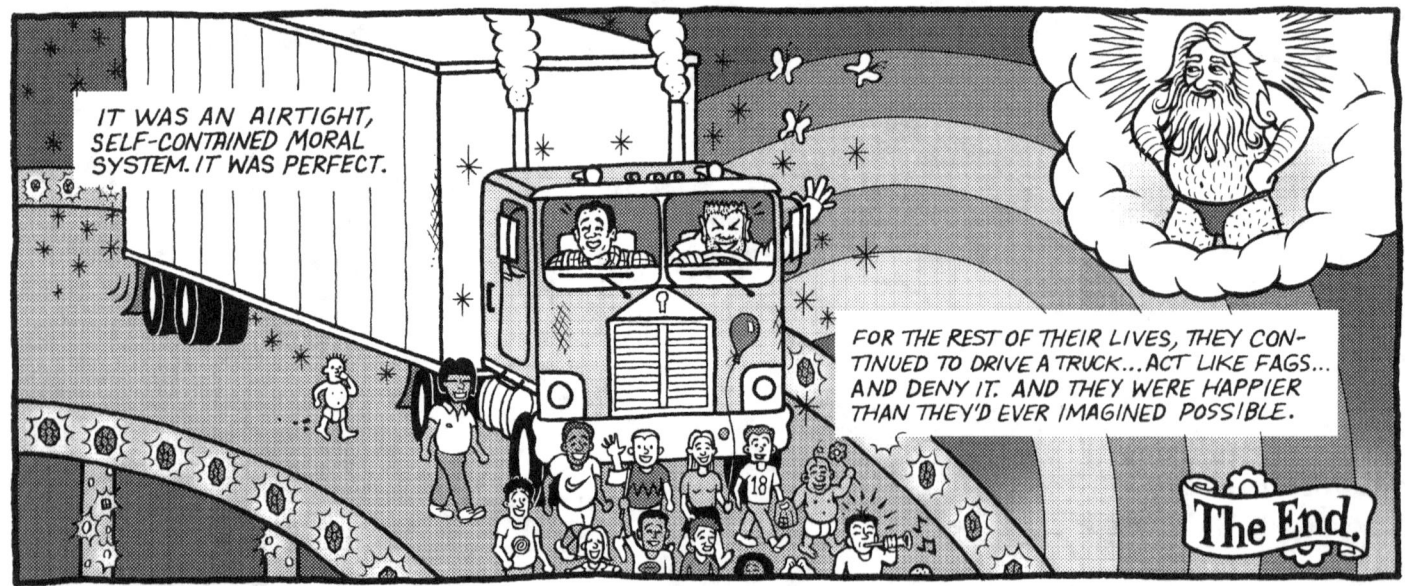

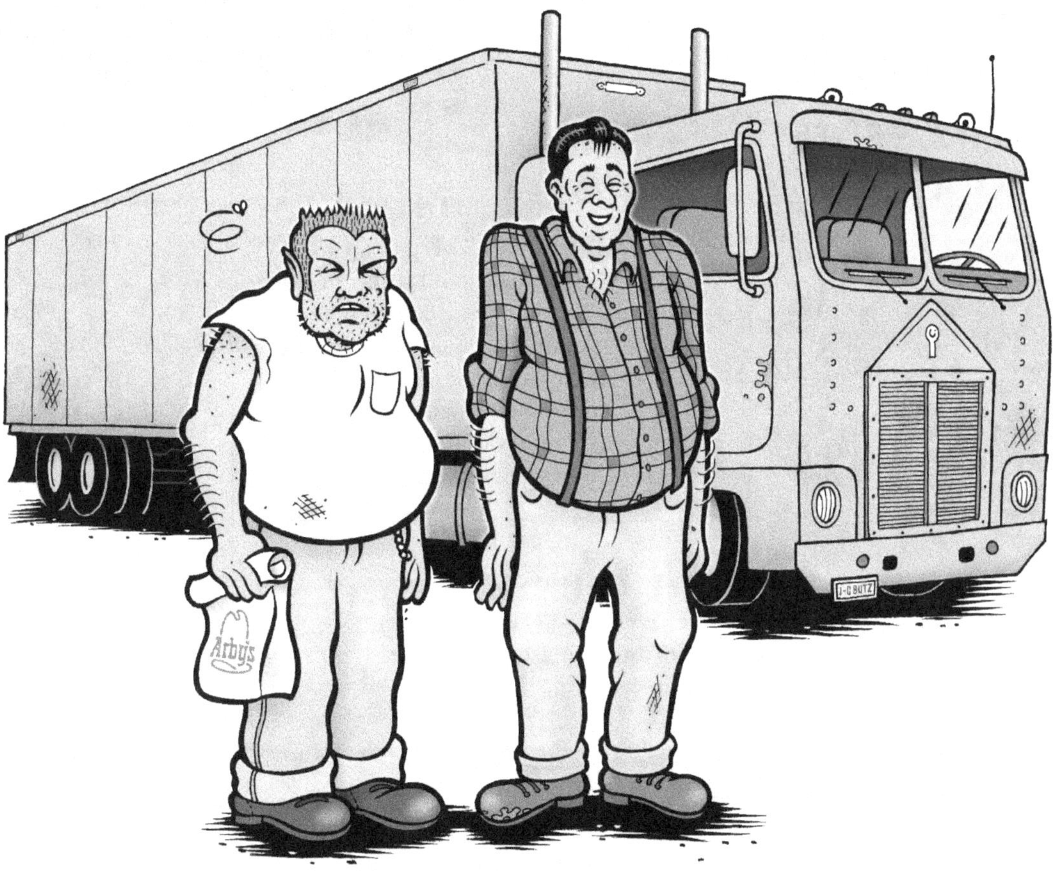

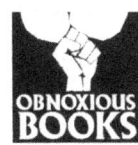

TRUCKER FAGS
IN DENIAL

Written by JIM GOAD · Art by JIM BLANCHARD

OBNOXIOUS
BOOKS

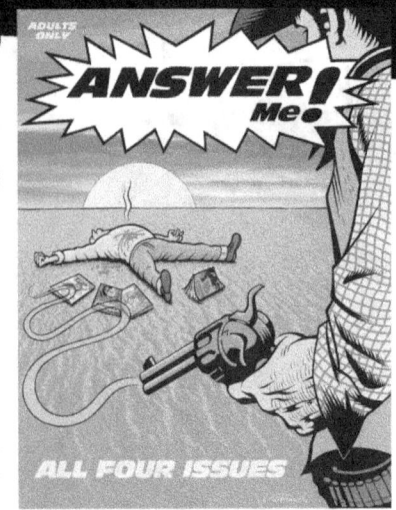
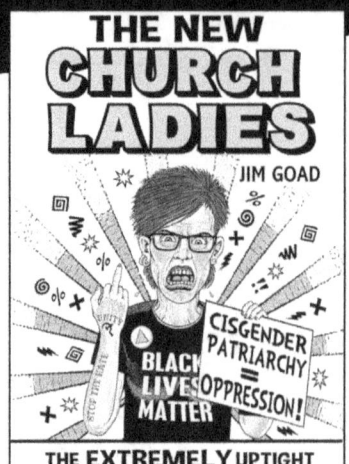
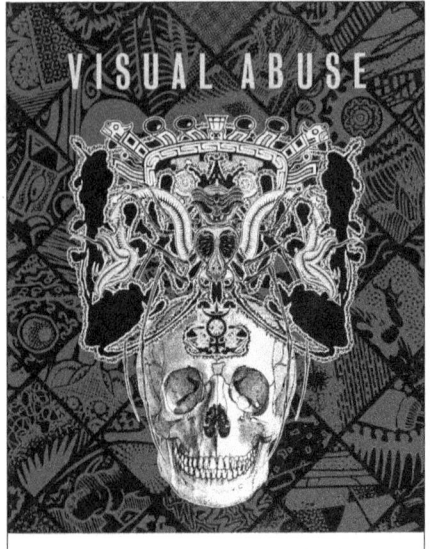